My Giants

My GIANTS

Russ Hodges

&

Al Hirshberg

DOUBLEDAY & COMPANY, INC., GARDEN CITY, NEW YORK

1963

To

EDDIE BRANNICK

who has been so good to baseball

My Giants

Chapter 1

In thirty years of broadcasting sports thrills, I've never been a big pill man. But at about two-fifteen on the afternoon of October 3, 1962, I had to take a tranquilizer to get through the ninth inning of the third game of the National League pennant playoff series between my beloved San Francisco Giants and the Los Angeles Dodgers. I got it from Charles S. (Chub) Feeney, the Giants' vice president, who was going crazy with me in the television booth at Dodger Stadium in Chavez Ravine.

People have been going crazy with me in radio and television booths ever since I joined the Giants in 1949. However, I had always avoided the tranquilizer bit, partly because I had always been younger than I was in the autumn of 1962, but mostly because I had never seen so much tension generated in such shattering silence. There were 45,693 people in that ball park, and they all seemed to have lost their larynxes.

I had to keep my voice down. This was not out of respect for stunned Los Angelenos who seemed aware that they were about to watch their favorites blow a pennant, but out of consideration for other announcers nearby and their listeners in various parts of the country. In our business, the cheers of a big crowd constitute background. When there aren't any cheers, the chattering of one loudmouthed visiting fireman in the next booth constitutes interruption. The distinction is fine, but unmistakable.

If I could have yelled into the microphone, as I did in

1951, when Bobby Thomson's home run gave the Giants of another era and another city a pennant of hallowed memory, I wouldn't have needed the tranquilizer. But Thomson hit his immortal blast in New York's Polo Grounds, then the Giants' home ball park. Since over thirty-four thousand fans were screaming in hysterical glee, I had to yell in order to be heard. A lucky thing, too, because there was nothing I wanted to do more.

That was my problem in Los Angeles. As the Giants began a ninth inning which I felt in my bones would result in another impossible victory for them, I wanted to yell like mad, but nobody else was yelling, so I had to stifle the impulse. When Matty Alou, batting for Don Larsen, led off with a single off Ed Roebuck, the Dodgers' pitcher, I couldn't stand it any longer. That's when I took the tranquilizer.

With the Giants two runs behind and facing a great team's best relief pitcher in his own backyard, a reasonable baseball fan would be justified in asking why I should get so excited over a simple leadoff base hit in the ninth inning. But I'm a Giants' fan, and there's nothing reasonable about a Giants' fan. His devotion to the ball club is unencumbered by logic. His faith is too strong to be shaken by the odds against his favorites, no matter how top-heavy they may be. He accepts mathematical elimination from the pennant race reluctantly, and considers anything short of it a better than even chance. As far as he is concerned, the Giants are dead only after they have been killed, and not one moment before.

Consider the events that had led up to this moment. On September 23, one week before the season ended, the Giants were four games behind the Dodgers with only seven games left to play. This was such a staggering lead at this late stage of the race that faith was all that could support even the vaguest Giants' hopes. The Dodgers would need only four

victories to clinch the pennant, even if the Giants went undefeated for the rest of the year, a highly unlikely prospect.
And for every game the Giants lost, the Dodgers would need
one less victory to win.

Giants' fans have been living off such meager morsels of
promise for years, and I could, too. When we beat Houston
and the Dodgers lost to St. Louis on the twenty-third, leaving us three behind with six games to go, I was positive we
couldn't lose.

On the airplane from Houston to San Francisco that night,
I told Lon Simmons, my broadcasting partner, "We're going
to win the pennant."

"I hope you're right," Lon said gloomily.

"I *know* I'm right," I said. "We finish at home."

"So do the Dodgers," he said.

"We play the Colts and the Cardinals," I said.

"So do the Dodgers," he said.

"Look, you big Indian," I said, "have faith."

"Fat man," he said, "I've got faith coming out of my ears.
But we're three games behind and the season ends Sunday.
Be reasonable."

He was right, of course. The idea that the Giants might
win was preposterous. But, as an older, more experienced
Giants' fan than Lon, I was convinced they would, anyway.

The twenty-fourth was an off day, and on the twenty-fifth
my blind faith showed signs of paying off when we beat the
Cardinals while the Dodgers were losing to the Colts. That
left us only two games behind with five to go. But the next
day both teams won, and the day after that both lost. This,
of course, helped the Dodgers. As long as we did what they
did they were all right. We couldn't win the pennant by
breaking even, but they could. We had to win while they
were losing—and if they didn't lose, we were dead.

September 26 was an off day for us, but we gained half a game because the Cardinals beat the Dodgers in Los Angeles.

Lon phoned that night and asked, "Fat man, what do you think?"

"I don't think," I said. "I know."

"Are we going to win?" he asked.

"Certainly," I said.

"A game and a half behind with two days left," he said. "I can't say I like the odds."

"Big Indian," I said, "there aren't any odds."

I was crazy, of course. The odds were huge, and we were on the short end.

The next day, we split a doubleheader with Houston while the Cardinals beat the Dodgers again. That took us into the last day of the season one game behind, and now the odds were heavier than ever against us. Even though we had won four out of six games and might win again, it was inconceivable that the Dodgers, who had lost five out of six, would keep on losing and that the Cardinals would keep on getting great pitching. Larry Jackson had beaten the Dodgers in ten innings for them one night and Ernie Broglio had thrown a two-hit shutout the next. How could we expect Curt Simmons, who was pitching for the Cardinals that day, to set the Dodgers back on their ears again?

But that was our only hope. If he didn't, we were finished. Even if he did, and we lost to the Colts, we were still finished. We had to win while the Dodgers were losing in order to tie for the pennant and force a playoff.

You had to be a complete Giants' nut to believe that such a thing could happen. I was and did.

It was Sunday afternoon, and Lon was broadcasting the San Francisco 49ers football game at Kezar Stadium, so I shared the Candlestick Park microphone with Bill King, who helped us on home games. Chub Feeney was sitting in the radio booth, as usual, along with our regular crew. The ball park was mobbed—if you included the freeloaders like ourselves, there were over forty-two thousand people there. They had come for the game, but an added lure was the fact that it was Fans' Appreciation Day. Afterwards, five lucky ticket-holders would get new cars, to be given out under the supervision of Walter Mails, a San Francisco baseball immortal who was head of our speakers' bureau.

Dick Farrell pitched for Houston, with Billy O'Dell going for the Giants. Ed Bailey belted a home run in the fourth to put us in the lead, but the Colts tied it up with three singles in the sixth. By that time, the Dodgers-Cardinals game had begun in Los Angeles—it started an hour behind our game —and from then on we were all leading a double life, with one eye on the field and the other on the scoreboard.

It was still 1–1 in San Francisco when Willie Mays came up in the last of the eighth. Even before he stepped into the batter's box, Lloyd Fox, the Candlestick Park organist, started to play, "Bye Bye Baby," the Giants' home run song. Willie was in a slump, having gone hitless his previous ten times at the plate.

He let the first pitch go by for a called strike, as the song died down. Then Farrell wound up and threw the second, and Willie kissed it. From the instant it left his bat, there was no question that it was gone, and I screamed, "Bye bye baby" before Lloyd had his pipes warmed up again.

That was the ball game.

Part of the miracle I had so confidently expected had now taken place, but we had to wait for the next part. The Dodgers and the Cardinals were in a scoreless tie at the end of the seventh. Somebody in our booth had managed to pick up

Vince Scully's account of the game direct from Los Angeles on a transistor radio, so I started passing it along to our own listeners.

"Don't leave us," I said. "The Giants won the ball game here, but they haven't won anything yet. We'll keep you up to date on how the Dodgers are doing. If they win, it's all over, but if they lose, there'll be a playoff here tomorrow. So stick around."

It was one of the most confusing broadcasts I ever made. Sometimes I had big gaps to fill, sometimes so much to say that I couldn't get it out fast enough. It wasn't easy to find out what was going on in Los Angeles. Everyone around me strained to hear Scully's voice through the squawking static from 350 miles away. All of us were plagued by the haunting thought that any minute we might lose it altogether.

In the meantime, the five shiny new cars to be given away were on the field in front of me, and Walter Mails was preparing to announce the winners over a special microphone set up near home plate. Nobody left the ball park, and the happy hum of hopeful Giants' denizens sounded like a huge turbine motor. There were transistor radios all over the place. I could see people holding them in their hands or up to their ears, so I knew I wasn't wasting my breath.

"One out for the Cardinals in the eighth," I said. "James just flied out and Gene Oliver is up . . ."

"And now for the first winner—" Walter Mails was speaking down on the field, and the crowd was hushed momentarily as he announced a park location by section, row, and seat. There was a flurry of handclapping and cheering, but I didn't pay much attention. I was too busy trying to fill up time.

"I want to congratulate Bill King—" I started, but I never finished the sentence because of what Scully was saying over the radio from Los Angeles. I couldn't believe my ears.

"He did what—?" I asked, in a stage whisper. "Just a minute—let's get that for sure—where did he hit it?"

Bill King had heard the same thing, and so had everyone else.

"Gene Oliver has just hit a home run into the left field stands to make it 1–0 in favor of the Cardinals!" I roared into the microphone.

There was an answering roar from those in the crowd who had radios, but that was nothing compared to the yell that went up when Jeff Carter, the park announcer, repeated the information over the loudspeaker. This was followed by another roar when a beautiful blonde stepped onto the field to claim a car she had just won.

"She's having trouble picking out the one she wants," I said over the air.

Then I remembered Bill King. He had just been named the announcer for the San Francisco Warriors basketball team, and had resigned from our crew. I wanted to give him a good sendoff.

I was right in the middle of that when someone handed me a set of instructions to fans on how to buy tickets for the playoff game, which would be held in Candlestick Park the next day if the Dodgers lost. There were also traffic instructions to read. By the time I was through, the Cardinals' half of the eighth inning was over in Los Angeles.

I used some of that time thanking our sponsors, Folger Coffee, the American Tobacco Company, and the Standard Oil Company of California, adding that they would sponsor the playoff games, if any.

Then the blonde picked a blue car, and I dutifully reported that. At this point, the Dodgers, behind 1–0, were up for

their half of the eighth, and I repeated Scully's announcement that Daryl Spencer was batting for Roseboro.

There was another time lag, so I started talking about the
1951 playoffs between the Dodgers and the Giants, but carefully listening for the action at Chavez Ravine, and stopping
to give it whenever there was any.

"Spencer just grounded out," I said. "That brings up Andy
Carey . . . We had a hiatus similar to this in 1951 . . . The
Giants thought they had it won . . . Carey just flied out . . .
That's two out in the Dodgers' eighth . . . Willie Davis is
up . . . Well, we took a train out of Boston figuring we
were home free, but . . . Davis grounded out, and the
Dodgers' eighth is over—a one, two, three inning for Curt
Simmons . . ."

I gave a pro football third-quarter score, and repeated the
special instructions for motorists, which gave me a chance
to plug one of our sponsors.

"Motorists," I said. "That's people who drive cars, and I
hope they use Chevron gas—"

I was losing interest in 1951, as the tension of the moment kept building up. What did anybody care what happened on a Boston–New York train when so much was going
on right here in California?

I halfheartedly finished the story, while Curt Flood flied
out and Stan Musial popped up to open the Cardinals' ninth.
Ken Boyer tripled, but was left there, and the Dodgers came
up for their own ninth, still trailing, 1–0.

"Our vice president, Charles S. Feeney, is sitting in the
booth with me here," I said over the air. "Are you thinking
about 1951, Chub?"

Chub looked at me, glassy-eyed, so I didn't press him for
an answer. Beads of perspiration were dancing on his fore-

head, and his vocal equipment was obviously paralyzed from the pressure. He was living in a dream world of his own.

"A gentleman is on the field to get a car from Walter Mails," I said, a little desperately, but I didn't push that point either. My heart wasn't in it. We were all waiting for Vince Scully to give us the start of the Dodgers' half of the ninth.

"Ken McMullen—a rookie—is pinch-hitting for Podres . . ." I let the microphone go dead, then as Scully spoke again, relayed the information that McMullen flied to Charley James for the first out.

"How are you enjoying life in the clubhouse, fellows?" I asked, knowing that the Giants were listening. "You're not nervous, are you? And how are you feeling, Lon?"

Lon, as it turned out, was having a rough afternoon, trying to listen to me and broadcast the football game at the same time. Every once in a while, he had to stop himself from saying that Mays made a tackle, or Kuenn threw a block, and once he actually did have Davenport gaining for the 49ers. There were probably as many transistor radios at Kezar as at Candlestick Park, and when something good for the Giants happened, the crowd roared for no reason apparent to the football players.

"Maury Wills has just flied to Charley James for the second out," I said. "Jim Gilliam will be the batter—with two down, bases empty, Cards leading, 1–0, last of the ninth . . .

"One strike to Gilliam—here's strike two, called . . ."

I wiped my forehead, took a deep breath, and said, "Boy, I'm glad my mother's here to prepare my padded cell. She's often wondered what's wrong with me. It's ball games and situations like this that can really hang you up to dry."

I'll never forget the scene in the radio booth, as we waited for word from Los Angeles. Chub Feeney was on his feet, pacing slowly back and forth, clenching and unclenching his fists, his eyes unblinking and round as saucers. Bill King sat silently on one side of me, while Franklin Mieuli, our producer, stared sightlessly out the window on the other. The rest were tense and quiet. The only sound was the clump of Feeney's shoes on the concrete deck and the metallic squall of the little transistor radio.

I cut the microphone and said, "Remember, fellows, we're on the air. No matter what happens, be careful what you say."

Nobody paid any attention. I switched myself back on the air, and leaned over to catch Vince Scully's voice.

Curt Simmons threw a low pitch, then Gilliam sliced a foul into the right field stands, and the count was two strikes and one ball.

"How are you feeling, Lon?" I said again. Then I screamed, *"He popped up to Javier—we have a playoff!"*

The words spilled out like air from a pricked balloon as the pressure broke. "The Cardinals beat the Dodgers, 1–0, and the Giants won, 2–1, so there'll be a playoff tomorrow—a playoff—a playoff! This is Russ Hodges—be back with us tomorrow for the Giants-Houston Colts—no—I mean the Giants-Dodgers game—no, I mean playoff . . ."

I finally got back on the track, and managed to finish the broadcast without any more bloops. In the meantime, Candlestick Park was going absolutely nuts. The place was a madhouse of shouting men and women dancing up and down the aisles, throwing whatever was handy, laughing, shaking hands, kissing, whacking each other on the back and making such a racket that they almost drowned out the joyous strains of "Bye Bye Baby," as Lloyd Fox banged it out over and over on the organ.

It wasn't long before we realized that the whole city of

San Francisco was going nuts. The sound of sirens, fire bells, auto horns, and all sorts of other noisemakers floated in from the outside. It was New Year's Eve in the afternoon, and the celebration continued through most of the night.

But, of course, the Giants hadn't won the pennant yet. They moved closer the next day when Billy Pierce shut out the Dodgers, 8–0, in the only playoff game at Candlestick Park, and then we all went to Los Angeles for the second game, and the third, if necessary.

I still wake up screaming in the night when I think of that second game. The Giants had a 5–0 lead in the sixth, and seemed on their way to an easy victory when the Dodgers, who hadn't scored a run in thirty-five innings, exploded for seven. They went on to score an 8–7 victory, which forced the playoffs into the third game.

Before it started, a reporter told Manager Alvin Dark of the Giants, who had been their shortstop in 1951 under the managership of Leo Durocher, "Durocher brought the same T-shirt he had worn in the 1951 playoff final. Did you bring any memento of that game?"

"Yeah," Dark replied. "Willie Mays."

Los Angeles was the only place from which we televised as well as broadcast ball games. Ordinarily, I was on TV and Lon on radio for the first three and the last three innings, and we swapped places for the middle three. The radio and television booths were about fifty feet apart at Dodger Stadium. By using taped and filmed commercials, we had plenty of time to make the switch between innings.

We also had the help that day of Harry Caray, the Cardinals' announcer, who had stayed over for the playoffs. He was in the radio booth, and volunteered to do whatever he could. As it turned out, we would have had a tough time getting along without him.

The Giants scored twice in the third on three Dodger errors, and had a 2–0 lead when Lon and I made our first change at the end of the inning. I thought I'd be on radio for three innings, but I lasted only one. After the Dodgers scored a run in the fourth to reduce the Giants' lead to 2–1, Lon suddenly elbowed me out of my seat.

"I'm a jinx on TV," he said. "You go back there, and I'll stay with radio."

I didn't argue. Lon had been on television during the Dodgers' seven-run sixth the day before.

But I wasn't any more help to the Giants than he had been. The Dodgers went into a 3–2 lead in the sixth on a two-run homer by Tommy Davis, and they added another run in the seventh when Maury Wills singled, stole second and third, and scored on a bad throw.

As the game moved into its final stages, the fans, either from smugness or apprehension, became quieter and quieter, and there was hardly a sound in the vast stadium when the Giants came to bat in the ninth. Maybe the Los Angeles people themselves had the same feeling I did—that something wonderful was about to happen to the Giants and something terrible to the Dodgers.

Whatever it was, there I sat wanting to yell, having to speak softly, and rapidly going out of my mind. Then Matty Alou hit his leadoff single, and I gulped the tranquilizer.

I thought those things worked right away, but this one didn't. When Harvey Kuenn forced Alou at second, my heart was pounding as hard as ever and my stomach was flipping like a stricken flounder. Then Roebuck walked Willie McCovey, batting for Chuck Hiller, and followed by passing Felipe Alou, too. That filled the bases with one out and Willie Mays at the plate.

The place was so quiet you could hear a pennant drop. I fought to keep my voice under control, while my nerves screamed for the relief of one uninhibited yell.

I turned toward Chub Feeney, pacing away behind me, and muttered, "The guy who made that tranquilizer must belong to the sugar trust. That's all he put into it."

Where Chub was, in his special dream world, he didn't hear me. Nobody did. Franklin Mieuli was on his feet, walking back and forth, and so was Bob Lurie. Mieuli was clenching his fists and mumbling to himself, and Lurie was wiping his face with a handkerchief. Neither paid any attention to me.

I shrugged and turned my attention back to the field, just in time to see Mays smash a murderous line drive off Roebuck's glove for a single. This could have been a double play but Kuenn scored and the others moved up, leaving the bases still full, and cutting the Dodger lead to 4–3.

Orlando Cepeda was the hitter, but Manager Walter Alston of the Dodgers was already out on the field to yank Roebuck and replace him with Stan Williams. While the pitching change was being made, I talked softly into the microphone and wished my leaping stomach would sit still long enough to digest the tranquilizer.

Williams was finally ready. Cepeda tied into a good pitch, lined out to the right fielder, and Ernie Bowman, running for McCovey, scored after the catch, and Alou went to third.

"It's tied up—" I spoke calmly, but my insides felt as if they were coming apart. I looked at Feeney, and he half-smiled, then lapsed back into his trance. Chub is never completely with us in a spot like that until the Giants actually go ahead.

"One more run," I said softly. "Just one more."

Mays went to second on a wild pitch, leaving first base

open, so Williams intentionally walked Ed Bailey. That brought up Davenport, with the bases full, two out, and the score tied.

In a faraway section of the stadium, somebody blew a da-da-da-da-da-*da* on a bugle, and a hardy group of Dodger fans followed it up with a hollow cheer which cut into the eerie silence. *"I wish I could do that,"* I thought bleakly.

I watched Davenport step into the batter's box, then, as the Dodger right-hander began pitching, my heart worked overtime again. *Williams couldn't find the plate.* He missed twice, then a third time, and finally a fourth. Davenport, recipient of the biggest base on balls of the season, trotted down to first, and Felipe Alou walked home with the run that put the Giants in front.

The rest was anticlimactic. Alston replaced Williams with Ron Perranoski, and the Giants scored another run on an error before the inning ended. That made it 6–4. Manager Alvin Dark sent in Billy Pierce, who had won the first game, to pitch the ninth for the Giants.

Pierce threw practically nothing but strikes. He fired two at Wills, who then grounded out. He threw two more at Gilliam before missing the plate with a low pitch, then Gilliam flied to Mays.

Now there were two out, and Lee Walls went up to bat for Larry Burright. The bugler came out with another blast, and his diehard chorus responded with a forlorn cheer about as inspiring as a leftover lamb chop. In the television booth, it was the only sound I heard.

Feeney was hardly breathing. Mieuli and Lurie stood rigid, their eyes riveted on the slim figure of Pierce. Charlie Einstein, the talented San Francisco free-lance writer who had covered the Giants for the *Examiner* the year before, had entered the booth. Usually relaxed and grinning, he was tense and serious, his face a mask of somber expectancy.

All of the Giants had come to the top of their dugout steps, where they crouched, poised to rush out and meet their teammates if all went well. Everyone was waiting for Pierce to dispose of Walls, the last obstacle in the way of the pennant.

The first pitch was a ball, the second a strike. Then Walls hit a harsh line drive toward center field, and Einstein said softly, "We're home."

He was quite right. Mays took a few steps, and slapped his glove with his bare hand, the signal that he knew he was going to catch the ball. In the same swift motion, he grabbed it, and fired it as far as he could into the right-field bleachers.

"He's got it," I yelled. *"The Giants win the pennant—the Giants win the pennant!"*

I signed off, knowing that I had to dash for the locker room for a combined radio and television broadcast from there. But I didn't feel like dashing. It seemed to me that I had all the time in the world.

The tranquilizer had taken hold at last.

I stopped at the radio booth, and there was Harry Caray, filling in the time it would take us to get set up downstairs. "Hodges and Simmons are on their way to the most hysterical clubhouse in America," he was saying.

Lon had already left. Harry looked at me and said, "Hi, Russ. What are you doing here?"

I grinned foolishly, and said, "I'm going down now." Then, with Franklin Mieuli tugging at my elbow, I started off, floating on the wings of Feeney's tranquilizer.

"Come on, Russ," Mieuli pleaded. "We've got to hurry."

"Don't worry, Franklin," I said. "We'll get there in plenty of time. Those guys will be celebrating for the next hour."

We finally walked into the noisy room, and got on the air. But just as I began to speak, somebody pulled the plug, and we were shut off.

While Mieuli frantically went to get us reconnected, I looked around, feeling like the keeper of Bedlam. This, I decided, must surely be the wildest locker room I had ever seen. I seemed to be the only calm man in a clubhouse jumping with screaming maniacs drenching each other with champagne, snapping wet towels at gleaming rumps, laughing, singing, leaping up and down, and acting generally as if they had just been released from the booby hatch.

Willie Mays came by, his eyes shining, his body glistening with the bubbles from a bottle somebody had emptied over his head. Orlando Cepeda was doing a cha-cha while Willie McCovey and Johnny Orsino beat time for him. Men were jumping on backs, throwing friendly punches, dancing around, diving in and out of the shower room, and whooping and laughing and shrieking and whistling and singing.

Now I felt cheated, for, no matter how hard I tried, I couldn't get excited. My heart went at a steady, normal beat, and my stomach felt fine, and I didn't know my nerves existed. I wished I hadn't taken that tranquilizer.

We finally got back on the air, and I started walking around with the microphone in my hand and the cord trailing along behind me. As Lon got the men lined up to speak, they calmed down enough to make sense while on television, then returned to their mad antics. But some were so emotionally spent they could hardly say anything. Felipe Alou, whose English isn't very good at best, stammered a few quivering words, and a deeply moved Juan Marichal quietly expressed his thanks to the Almighty.

I went from man to man—to Cepeda and McCovey and Davenport and Kuenn and Hiller and Haller and Pagan and

Sanford and Pierce and all the rest. I talked to Alvin Dark and, after he got the champagne off, to Willie Mays.

In the meantime, I was sure the program, which was supposed to last fifteen minutes, was running overtime. Mieuli normally gave me the signal to get off the air, but I couldn't find him. I finally signed off without him. Later, I learned that we had run seven minutes late, but the sponsors were so happy the Giants had won that they didn't care.

I broke up when I found out what happened to Mieuli. Willie McCovey had poured a bottle of champagne over his head, and it had streamed into his contact lenses. The poor guy couldn't even see his watch, let alone my chubby figure.

The daffy party ended at last, and soon we were on the airplane for San Francisco and the opening of the World Series. It was the first time since the game was over that I had a chance to talk to Lon alone.

"Well, big Indian," I said, "what do you think now?"

"Fat man," he said, "I think you were right all the time. I'll never lose faith again."

"You're making progress," I said. "Give yourself about thirty-five years and you'll be up to me. That's how long I've been a Giants' fan."

"You wasted a lot of years not being one, didn't you, fat man?" he said.

"And I regret every single one of them," I said.

Chapter 2

My mother always hoped I'd be a successful singer, and if you ask Lon Simmons, that's just what I became. "When Russ sings 'Danny Boy,'" Lon says, "we all sit around and cry a lot." If that's not being a successful singer, what is?

I was born on June 18, 1910, in Dayton, Tennessee. That was the site, fifteen years later, of the world-famous "monkey trial" of John T. Scopes for teaching evolution, but we were long gone by then. As a matter of fact, I don't remember Dayton at all, because our family, which included my parents, my older brother, and me, moved to Danville, Kentucky, when I was very small.

It was there that I first became a red-hot sports fan. Centre College, which had but 270 students, built up one of the great football teams of its time. Led by the immortal Bo McMillan, the "Praying Colonels," as they were known, beat mighty Harvard in 1921, after having lost an exciting 31–14 game to the Crimson the year before.

While I wasn't on the premises long enough to help celebrate the 1921 victory, I was the team's water boy in 1920, and Centre's stars, McMillan, Red Weaver, and Red Roberts, were my first sports heroes. At one time or another, all three made Walter Camp's All-America team, quite a distinction in a day when Camp made a substantial number of his selections from the Ivy League.

My father, a telegrapher for the Southern Railroad, was a fan of tremendous proportions. He would travel miles to see a major sports event. In 1919, when I was nine years old, he took me to Toledo for the Dempsey-Willard heavyweight championship fight, and I was a boxing nut from then on. I still enjoy a good brawl, although I don't have the opportunity to go to many.

In the late autumn of 1920 we moved to Covington, Kentucky, across the Ohio River from Cincinnati, and that's where I really grew up. When anyone asks me where I got my hominy and 'tater accent, I tell them Covington, but of course that's only technically in the South. All I ever knew about the Deep South was what my mother told me. To this day, you can hear the strains of "Dixie" in her voice, for she was raised far below the Mason-Dixon Line.

"Son," she used to drawl, in tones dripping with moonlight and magnolias, "the only kind of a girl for you is a real southern belle. When you see that black hair and those rosy cheeks and red lips, and when you fall under the spell of those flashing dark eyes, and when you hear that lovely voice, you won't ever want to look at another girl. Nobody in this whole world has the carriage and the pride and the dignity and the beauty and the culture and the background and the upbringing of a true southern belle. Just wait until you meet one."

I had to wait a long time, because we didn't seem to have any around Covington, Kentucky. That was too far north for Mother. I didn't do much traveling in the South until years later, when I became a sports announcer. I was married by then, but I still kept my eyes open for the feminine paragon of my mother's description. If I ever saw her, I'd speak to her, just to hear her talk.

It got to be quite a search, because real southern belles were scarce around ball parks and railroad stations even in the heart of Dixie. I traveled in and out of Florida and through the cotton belt for years before I ran into one.

It happened in Atlanta, Georgia—the most natural place in the world to find the real McCoy in belles. There was a pretty big crowd at the ball park, and people were still filing out by the time I had signed off my broadcast.

As I started down one aisle, I saw the girl of Mother's dreams making her way down another. She was a vision in a white angora sweater and blue skirt, and she looked exactly as my mother pictured her. Beside her was a tall, thin youth with sensitive features and the proud bearing of a Confederate officer.

They weren't going very fast, so it was easy for me to rush down my aisle, go out the nearest gate, and turn back so I would be approaching them from the front instead of the rear. A full-view look at the girl confirmed the soundness of my mother's judgment. She was about nineteen years old, and her face and figure practically screamed breeding and class.

She and her escort sauntered toward me without speaking. For a moment, I thought I'd have to say something to get a word out of her, but this wasn't necessary. Just as the couple came abreast of me, the boy belched.

My Scarlett O'Hara turned on him and, in a voice like congealed honey, snarled, "Randolph—are you going to puke again?"

Mother's zeal in getting me to appreciate the virtues of southern belles was more than matched by her efforts to make a concert singer out of me. She failed, of course, but that wasn't her fault.

She sang beautifully, and passed along both to my brother and me her love for good music. During my adolescence, the opera names of Caruso, Schumann-Heink, Galli-Curci, Scotti, Farrar, and Patti were as familiar to me as the baseball names of Roush, Donohue, Rixey, Eller, Groh, Daubert, Moran, and the rest of the Cincinnati Reds of that era.

We had a gramophone that you wound up before putting a record on, and a collection of classical records, all of which would be museum pieces today. The records were made of hard rubber, thick and easily breakable, and blank on one side. They didn't improve with age. After a while, the wonderfully rich tones of the incomparable Caruso sounded like the scratching of hen's feet on a window pane.

My brother had a fine tenor voice and really liked to sing. Despite my mother's encouragement, he never tried to make it professionally, any more than I did. I was a pretty good barroom baritone, but that was enough to convince Mother where my future lay. A few years after my voice changed, she sent me to the Cincinnati College of Music, where I took lessons under a singing instructor named Fenton Pugh. His name belied his talents, for he was really very good, but he couldn't make a silk purse out of a sow's ear. I just didn't have it.

But for a while we talked classical music around the house until my poor father nearly went out of his mind. I ran through my scales under the shower every day, and mi-mi-mi-ed off in corners, and when I practiced nobody was allowed near me.

"Shh," my mother used to say. "Don't bother Russell. Some day we'll be hearing him at the Metropolitan."

"He'll be an athlete," my father used to retort. "That's what he really wants."

Of course he was right, but I didn't mind the voice practice, and it pleased my mother. What little interest I had soon ran its course, and Mr. Pugh and I parted company. I preferred to concentrate on third base in the spring and summer, and the backfield in the fall.

No sports-minded kid could grow up in Covington without being a Reds' fan. Their shining star was Edd Roush, who for years held forth in center field with grace and distinction. Besides being a marvelously smooth outfielder, he was a consistent .300 hitter, and twice won the National League batting championship. Because he hated spring training, he was a chronic holdout. He always waited until the team started home from the South before signing his contract. In the process, he usually succeeded in coaxing a substantial salary raise. That got to be such a serious business with him that he once held out all season because the front office wouldn't satisfy his financial demands.

As far as I was concerned, you could have the Babe Ruths and Ty Cobbs and George Sislers and Rogers Hornsbys and all the rest. There was nobody like Edd Roush, and I faithfully lived and bled and died with the Reds as long as he played for them. One of my life's more satisfactory moments came in 1962, when, after years of denial, Roush finally won proper recognition for his feats by being named to baseball's Hall of Fame. I could think of no one who deserved it more.

To my horror, Roush was traded to the Giants in January of 1927. Then, since my adoration for Roush was deeper than my loyalty to the Reds, I shifted my allegiance to the Giants, and they've had me ever since.

I was a better singer than a baseball player, but I didn't do badly in football. As a chunky halfback, I made enough of a name for myself locally to get a football scholarship at the University of Kentucky. This was a source of great satisfaction to my father. My mother, while she would have preferred it to be a voice scholarship, was pleased at the opportunity for me to obtain a college education.

But my gridiron ambitions practically collapsed when I cracked an ankle in the first game of my sophomore year. It wasn't a bad break, but enough to keep me out of football for the rest of the year. Actually, it turned out to be a good break, for it led me indirectly into the broadcasting booth.

When Kentucky played Tennessee at Lexington one day, Station WHAS of Louisville sent George Wederhold, its program director, to broadcast the game. I knew all the Kentucky players, so I spotted for him. Wederhold was a music expert, familiar with glissandis and crescendos, but unable to tell an off-tackle play from a naked reverse. He stumbled through the first half so badly that the station was deluged with phone calls from indignant fans.

During the half-time intermission, Wederhold said, "Russ, did you ever broadcast before?"

"No, sir," I said.

"Well," he said, "you've got a good voice and you know what this game is all about. How about doing the second half?"

That was the first time I ever sat behind a microphone. I'd like to report that I was so sensational that WHAS was swamped with more calls, demanding that that fine young Russ Hodges be put to work there permanently, but nothing like that happened. In those days nobody was interested in any sports announcers except Ted Husing and Graham McNamee, and I was no threat to either. But at least the complaints stopped.

I played football again the following year, but mostly as a sideline performer. I had the cleanest uniform on the field and was the first man off the bench to cheer when we scored a touchdown. Mr. Pugh might not have found a use for my rich baritone, but it led all the rest in cheering at Kentucky and gave me a certain distinction among my teammates.

My big chance to play came late in the season, when the team went to Eddyville for the annual joust with the state penitentiary team. Since this came on an off-Saturday just before the Tennessee game, the regulars were saved, because the coach didn't want any of them to get hurt. Only expendables like me made the trip.

The setup at State Pen was the answer to a coach's dream. There was no alumni problem and no three-year varsity restriction. Everybody always showed up for practice, and nobody loafed on the field. Furthermore, the team had the biggest scouting corps in the state, since every cop in Kentucky helped to recruit ballplayers.

Maybe because he thought I was entitled to some recognition for all my enthusiasm, Coach Harry Gamage of Kentucky named me captain of the team. I was the tailback of a single-wing offense, and the prospect of carrying the ball often had me all steamed up.

The first time I took it, I hadn't gone three steps when I was belted to a fare-thee-well. The next thing I knew, I was looking up into the grizzly face of a grinning gargoyle who smothered me with an overpowering fragrance of garlic on his breath. The guy was a man of monumental proportions, a homely giant badly in need of a shave. Just before he let me up, he dug an elbow into my ribs.

Later, when I got back to the bench after having spent more time under this character than opposite him, I learned that his name was Laughing Boy McGee, and I don't mind telling you he frightened me to death. He stood six feet, five inches and weighed 275 pounds. The only advantage I had over him was youth, for he was about twice my age.

After a while, Laughing Boy tore so many of us apart that nobody wanted to carry the ball. At the end of the first half, we had a net loss from scrimmage of forty-four yards, and the game was tied at 0–0.

Gamage was fit to be tied himself. "You fellows ought to be ashamed of yourselves," he said between the halves. "You're supposed to be fighting Kentuckians, and you're letting a bunch of old men beat your brains out. Now go back there and do a job."

It was a great pep talk, but not enough to offset Laughing Boy or his unbelievable breath. When he didn't knock us down, he blew us down. The only chance we'd ever have to win the ball game was to stay out of his way, but this was impossible. There was no place on the field where you could escape from him.

I hoped that somebody could avoid him at least enough to carry the ball into Pen's territory so we might have a chance to score. It happened late in the game, when one of our boys grabbed a punt and ran it all the way to their eighteen-yard line. That was enough to fire me up to the heights of bravery.

"Gimme the ball!" I growled in the huddle.

So they gave me the ball, and I churned back almost to the scrimmage line before I ran into Laughing Boy. He elbowed me as he brought me down, and kneed me in the stomach before he let me up.

That was too much. Mad and frustrated, I jumped to my feet, rose to my full height of five feet, eight inches, looked him right in the belly button, and snapped, "What are you in here for?"

Without changing the silly smile on his ugly face, he blew a full head of garlic at me and said, "Killing a fat little slob exactly like you."

That did it. I had neither the strength nor the will to carry the ball again. My dreams of glory collapsed, and so did my football career. I stayed around long enough to cheer the varsity on to a 6–6 tie against Tennessee the following week, and then turned in my uniform.

That, of course, was the end of my football scholarship, but I finished out the year, picking up a few dollars on odd jobs and occasionally getting a chance to broadcast a college sports event. The next year, back home in Covington, I entered law school at the University of Cincinnati nights and looked for a daytime job that would put me through.

I knew L. B. Wilson, the manager, and Maurice Thompson, the program director, of WCKY, which was then in Covington, but is now a Cincinnati station. Wilson let me do what few sports programs he used. One day he said, "Russ, how would you like to handle our early-morning show?"

"How early?" I asked.

"Start at five-thirty," he said. "We've got a great audience of farmers and early risers who love hillbilly music. You play the records part of the time and talk the rest."

"How much?" I asked.

"Twenty a week," he said. "If you do a good job, I'll make it twenty-two-fifty and maybe eventually get you up to twenty-five."

So I became the cheerful little early bird of WCKY, and, incidentally, an expert on hillbilly music. We played classics like "The Judge Said 'Stand Up Boy and Dry Your Tears, You're Sentenced to Nashville for Twenty-One Years,'" and "My Horses Ain't Hongry, They Won't Eat Your Hay," and other such rural tear-jerkers.

We had some wonderful characters on the air—the Tennessee Ramblers, the Cumberland Crooners, Ramblin' Red Foley, the Hill-billy Kid, Asher Sizemore, and the Georgia Skillet-Lickers. Foley is still one of the stars of our country music television shows, while the others have had their days of glory.

"All right," I used to say, as the sun was coming up, "let's all listen to some of that good old fiddlin' music," and I'd put on "Seven Years with the Wrong Woman." When it was over, I'd talk awhile about the mountain music we all loved so well, and maybe read a news item or two from the morning paper. (In those days—around 1930—radio wire services were unheard of, so we had to depend on the newspapers.) Then perhaps I'd spin, "The Dream of a Miner's Child," or "She'll Be Coming 'Round the Mountain," and go through the routine all over again.

The sounds of the hills didn't bother me in the slightest, but they gave my mother the screaming meemies. I really couldn't blame her for her annoyance at this turn in my career. It was only a few years before that she had been hearing me do my scales and mi-mi-mi-ing all around the house, with one foot in the door of La Scala, and now here I was directing a barn dance every morning.

She stood it as long as she could, then demanded, "Can't you do something else?"

"Like what?" I asked.

"Go to work for the railroad, like your father and your brother," she said.

"I'd have to work all day then," I said. "I'd be too tired to go to law school at night."

"I suppose that's so," she said. "Anyhow, please promise me you'll give up that awful program after you pass the bar," she said.

"I will if I can," I said, "but I can't give it up now."

Another time, she came home badly upset.

"What's the matter?" I asked.

"Well," she said, "on the streetcar today I heard a couple of people arguing, and one finally got real mad and said, 'I hope all your children grow up to be radio announcers.' You can imagine how that made me feel."

I grinned.

"It's an old gag," I said. "It's really not so bad being a radio announcer."

She phoned the station one day and said, "Russell, get over to Mr. Green's butcher shop as fast as you can."

"Why?" I asked.

"He's got an opening," she said, "and he promised he'd give it to you if you go after it today."

"Tell him to give it to somebody else," I said. "I don't want to be a butcher."

By then, the Great Depression of the thirties had set in, and Mother finally realized I was lucky to have a job at all. But she never quite reconciled herself to the hillbilly program. She was afraid somebody from the Cincinnati College of Music would hear it, and I'd be ostracized from the alumni.

In 1932, we started broadcasting Reds' games direct from the ball park, and, to my mother's infinite relief, I was finally off the mountain music program. At that time, nobody worried about sponsors or exclusive broadcasting rights, and the ball club was glad to have us. After all, it was selling baseball, and here we were dishing it out for anyone who happened to have a radio on.

The job delighted me, largely because I got paid for going to the ball park. I collected twenty-five dollars a week, which wasn't bad, considering the hours. There weren't any night games. I just worked afternoons, starting when the game began, and finishing when it ended. I also did an early evening show. While the club was on the road, I worked around the station, doing news and sports programs, and making myself generally useful.

But, no matter how hard I tried, I couldn't put over commercials well. Every time one was given me to read, it came up in my throat. I stammered around, and when I finally got the words out, I sounded about as convincing as a schoolboy reciting *Hiawatha.* I couldn't sell catsup to a bean eater. It took me years to improve even a little, but I never was a hotshot, and I'm still one of the worst readers of commercials in the business.

In 1933, the same year that Larry MacPhail came to the Reds, I graduated from law school and passed the bar. Now I really had to make a decision. Lawyers were jumping out of windows like flies, and young ones were lucky to get office space. Salaries were unheard of. A fledgling lawyer started out working for experience, and if he showed any promise he might get ten dollars a week after a while.

To give up a paying job I loved for this seemed ridiculous to me. Besides, I already had heavy responsibilities. I was married and my son, Pat, had just been born. I couldn't afford to quit.

But MacPhail was giving the station a hard time. WCKY was so powerful it could be heard in the Pittsburgh area, and the Pirates didn't like it. They complained to the Reds, and MacPhail finally barred us from the ball park. While this didn't cost me my job, it was a serious blow to my ambitions of becoming a big-time sports announcer, and I immediately began looking around for an opening.

After several months, I heard about one in Rock Island, Illinois, that paid thirty dollars a week, five more than I was getting. Rock Island, of course, was hardly the big time, but I wouldn't be handling anything else but sports events. There were two Three-I League teams, the Rock Island Rocks and the Davenport Blue Sox, so I'd always have a ball game to do during the baseball season, and I'd have the University of Iowa football games, too.

Even though it was a better opportunity than the job I had, I hesitated about leaving the major leagues for the bushes. I finally decided that if WCKY would match the salary raise Rock Island offered, I'd stay.

So I went to L. B. Wilson, my boss, and said, "How about a raise to thirty a week?"

"A raise, Russ?" he said. "Did you say a raise? Do you realize what year this is?"

"Sure," I said. "Nineteen thirty-four."

"Do you realize we're in the depths of the worst depression we've ever known?" he demanded.

I squirmed. "Yeah," I said. "I know."

"And you still want a five-dollar raise?"

"Yes, sir," I said.

He glared at me for several minutes. Then he said, "You want to know something, Hodges? I can walk down any dark alley any night with my shotgun, shoot it at random, and hit forty better sports announcers than you'll ever be."

"Go ahead and shoot," I said. "I'm through."

And I walked out.

I didn't spend a full year in Rock Island. One Sunday night, right after the football season of 1934 ended, I found a note on my desk at the station, where I had gone to do an evening sports show.

"If you're interested in working in Chicago," it said, in effect, "I'll be glad to talk to you any time."

It was signed by Ralph Atlass, owner of station WIND. By the time he walked into his office Monday morning, I was waiting for him.

"I caught your last football broadcast and liked it," he said. "I need a man to do all kinds of sports—baseball, football, boxing, Kelly pool—anything you can think of. The job is yours if you want it."

I didn't even ask about salary. I accepted on the spot.

It marked the beginning of a fine association with a wonderful guy, to say nothing of some of the most valuable radio experience of my life.

Chapter 3

Chicago was wide open in all other respects, so it shouldn't have been a surprise to me that there were almost no radio restrictions there either. But I must admit it was something of a shock to find the press boxes at Comiskey Park and Wrigley Field crawling with play-by-play announcers. There was nothing exclusive about my new job. I was one of five different guys sitting behind five different microphones broadcasting over five different stations. We worked side by side, so close together that we never had to worry about dead air. No matter which station they tuned, the fans could always hear somebody talking.

Both the White Sox and the Cubs welcomed us all with open arms. Unlike Cincinnati, which was within radio range of Pittsburgh, we didn't interfere with any other major league city. The two Chicago ball clubs figured there was enough air for everybody, and anyone who wanted to set up a microphone in the press box was at liberty to do so—the more, the merrier, in fact. As a result, in 1935 and the years immediately following, Chicago had the wildest baseball broadcasting jamboree in the history of the game or the industry.

Nobody knew for sure who had the biggest audience, but Pat Flanagan of WBBN seemed to be the leader, judging by the volume of his mail, his phone calls, and the general reaction to his comments. Bob Elson of WGN, who still does White Sox games, wasn't far behind him, and the other two, John Harrington and Hal Totten, each had followings of their own.

That didn't leave much for poor old Russell Patrick Hodges, who stepped into this mare's nest unknown and unsung, representing the newest and smallest of the five baseball stations. WIND was just getting started then, and Atlass hoped to build it up as a sports station.

Baseball was a glut on the Chicago radio market, but it was better than nothing. The afternoon hours were considered practically useless at that time. Housewives were supposed to sit home and listen to their radios in the morning, but it was assumed they had other things to do after lunch. Automobile radios were considered a luxury and transistors hadn't been invented yet. The afternoon was the dullest time of the day, with the exception, of course, of the hours between one and six in the morning.

Baseball was used to fill this gap because that gave the stations something to sell. The salesmen reached all over the country in their frantic search for sponsors, and they were willing to peddle the time for a song.

Our own case was typical. Our sponsors were the Penn Tobacco Company of Wilkes-Barre, Pennsylvania, makers of Kentucky Club Tobacco and Kentucky Winner Cigarettes. For the entire 1935 season of 154 games, they paid us a grand total of $18,000, or about $120 a game. The price included the time, setting up of telephone lines, an engineer, and Hodges, and nobody considered it a bargain. Today, the would-be sponsor with a bankroll of $18,000 for a baseball program couldn't get beyond the station manager's secretary.

Our guarantee of 154 games meant 154 games, not 153 or 152. If there was no game in Chicago, we had to bring one in from the outside via telegraphic re-creation, and I was spared that ordeal only when every team in both major leagues was idle. Telegraphic re-creations were an invention of the devil, but I lived with them for years. I still do one every so often, but I don't like it any better now than I did nearly thirty years ago.

A telegraphic re-creation must be part fact—what happens in the ball game—and part fiction—what the announcer can invent to fill up the gaps. Not being on the spot, since he works in his home studio, the announcer has to draw liberally on his imagination. He sits beside a telegraph operator on whom he is dependent for every morsel of hard news. In my Chicago days, all the operators used Morse code, which they typed in plain English exactly as it came in.

To save wire tolls, the information was confined to the barest essentials. It was sent in standard baseball shorthand. If the announcer repeated only what came in, he'd lose his audience in ten minutes and his job in fifteen.

He got such information as the lineups and batting orders, the umpires, the weather and a crowd estimate, followed by the progress of the game, pitch by pitch. From these little acorns, he had to build an oak tree of delineation.

In 1935, a typical first half inning between the Cubs and the Cardinals in St. Louis would look like this as it came over the wire:

"Galan up . . . S 1 C. B 1. S 2 F. B 2 . . . 7 . . . Herman up . . . B 1. S 1. S 2 C . . . 4–3. Hartnett up . . . S 1. B 1 . . . Singles 7 . . . Demaree up . . . S 1. B 1. B 2. S 2 C . . . 8 . . . 1–0–0–1."

In straight English this meant:

"Galan up . . . Strike one called. Ball one. Strike two foul. Ball two . . . Flies out to left (7) . . . Herman up . . . Ball one. Strike one. Strike two called . . . Grounds out, second to first (4–3). Hartnett up . . . Strike one. Ball one . . . Singles to left (7) . . . Demaree up . . . Strike one. Ball one. Ball two. Strike two called . . . Flies out to center (8) . . . One hit, no runs, no errors, one left."

To the casual baseball fan, nothing could sound duller than that, except, perhaps, the clacking of the telegraph "bug" and the clattering of the typewriter in the background. In order to dress it up, I would say something like this:

"It's a beautiful, sunny day at Sportsman's Park in St. Louis, as Paul Dean finishes his warmups. The Cardinals' right-hander rubs up the ball and looks around the infield, and Augie Galan steps to the plate. Galan, a switch-hitter, bats from the left side against Dean . . ."

By this time, the ball game has started, and a couple of pitches have already been called on Galan. But when you have to talk steadily, it's always better to let the action pile up, because each little symbol that comes over the wire can give you material for fifty to a hundred words. I might continue the broadcast this way:

"Dean leans forward for the sign, nods his head, and goes into his windup. His arms come down, and he burns a fast ball right across the letters. Galan lets it go by, and Umpire Dolly Stark calls it a strike. The ball goes back to Dean, and he kicks at the rubber. He hitches up his pants, takes a glance around the infield, gets his sign, and winds up again. It's inside and low, and Galan lets it go by for ball one.

"Now it's one and one, and Dean is getting ready to pitch again. Paul is in good form this afternoon, fresh and strong, and he's all arms and legs as he goes into his windup . . . Galan swings . . . *and fouls it off* . . . a *vicious* line drive into the upper deck in right field. Boy, he sure got a piece of that fast ball inside, and now there's a scramble among the fans for the ball . . . Oops, there's an usher racing against three kids. One of the boys has it now, and holds it up for everyone to see. The crowd cheers, and turns back to the ball game . . ."

Now I'd be perhaps two batters ahead of the action, so I could relax a bit. Between having him look around the infield, hitch up his pants, get his signs from the catcher and do all the other hundred and one things pitchers are likely to do, I could keep Paul Dean out on that mound for five extra minutes, and in a telegraphic re-creation, five minutes is pure gold. It might put an announcer two or three plays ahead of the action.

The fans seemed to enjoy the whole performance, even though they knew it was all coming out of my head. As a matter of fact, we didn't try to fool anyone. We always announced in advance, and several times during the broadcast as well, that the game was coming by wire from another city. But it was a job that taxed the imagination, and, besides, I much preferred watching a ball game to looking over a telegrapher's shoulder.

The five Chicago announcers didn't always agree, and the baseball writers got a kick out of calling attention to the different ways in which each of us sometimes called a play. We all saw everything from exactly the same angle, since our seats were along the third-base line. This gave us a better view of the right-field foul line than the umpires had. As a result, I got into a fine mess only a few months after I went to work for WIND in 1935.

One afternoon at Wrigley Field, the Cubs were in a close game with the Cardinals, and put on a rally in the last of the eighth. With men on second and third and two out, Kenny O'Dea, a fine young catcher, came up as a pinch-hitter. He hit a line drive down the right-field line and, as the crowd roared, I watched to see where it would land.

"Foul by a foot," I announced, then glanced down at my scorecard. When I looked up, O'Dea was sliding into third base and two runs were home.

"Oh, my," I said. "I made a mistake. Umpire Magerkurth called it fair, and O'Dea has a triple."

George Magerkurth, a huge man with a stentorian voice, was a tough old bird who called plays as he saw them, and he didn't always see them the way everyone else did. He was involved in some famous brawls. Once, he and Billy Jurges had a spitting contest in Brooklyn. Another time, a fan came out of the stands to take a swing at him. Mage was a real nice guy off the field, but on it he was positive, dogmatic, and uncompromising.

As it happened, all of the other four announcers also had called O'Dea's hit a foul, and the next day the press had a field day.

"They don't agree often," one writer said, in effect, "and when they do, it's a good bet they'll be as wrong as they were yesterday."

The Chicago newspapers took their baseball so seriously that the home team was almost always on page one, and only a blind non-fan could have missed stories about the incident. Judge Kenesaw Mountain Landis, then the baseball commissioner, was neither blind nor a non-fan, and his office was in Chicago. I was just sitting down for breakfast when I got a call from there.

"The judge wants to see you at one o'clock," said Leslie O'Connor, his top assistant.

"I'll be there," I said.

I hardly looked forward to the interview. I had been introduced to the old gentleman a couple of times, and he scared me to death. With his beetle brows, his snow-white hair, his ice-blue eyes, his stern visage, and his deep voice, he scared everybody to death.

My knees actually shook as I walked into his spacious suite at 333 Michigan Avenue.

"Take a seat, Mr. Hodges," O'Connor said, kindly. "The judge will be with you in a minute."

Promptly at one, I was ushered into the presence. Judge Landis was sitting behind a huge desk, reading some papers. He let me stand and shift my feet for several moments before he looked up, glared at me, and thundered, "You're Hodges?"

"Yes, sir," I stammered. "I'm Russ Hodges."

"What religion are you, Hodges?"

"I'm a Baptist, sir," I said.

"You're a pretty lousy Baptist, aren't you?" he said.

"Well—I don't get to church as often as I should," I said, "so I guess I am."

"What do you know about baseball?" he demanded.

"A little," I said.

"But not much."

"No, sir," I said, "not much."

"How much money have you ever spent to watch ball games?" he asked.

"Well," I said, "when I was a kid—"

"Sure," he said, "when you were a kid, you sneaked into the park, or if you paid your way you sat in the bleachers."

"Yes, sir."

"You see pretty good ball games every day, don't you, Hodges?"

"Yes, sir."

"And it doesn't cost you a dime, does it?"

"No, sir."

"You're in on a perpetual rain check."

"Yes, sir."

The judge leaned forward. "Hodges," he said, "what makes you think you know more about the game than George Magerkurth?"

I stood, miserable and perspiring, and said nothing.

"What were you doing in 1888?" he asked.

"I wasn't born yet," I said.

"Well, Magerkurth was," he said. "How old were you in 1922?"

"Twelve."

"Magerkurth was umpiring then," he said. "Do you think you know as much about baseball as he does?"

"No, sir," I said.

"Do you think you know as much about baseball as *any* big league umpire?"

"No, sir."

"Well, Hodges," he said, "I know you have to go out and broadcast a ball game this afternoon. When the minister in your Baptist church preaches a sermon, and he says, 'The Good Lord saved the children of Israel from the fiery furnace,' what do you say?"

"I say, 'Amen,' Judge," I said.

"And the next time Magerkurth calls a foul ball fair, what are you going to say?"

"Amen," I said.

"Right," he said. "Now get out of here and go broadcast your ball game."

Chapter 4

The tower of babel into which I landed in 1935 was doomed, although none of us realized it at the time. Advertising experts who had stuck up their noses at afternoon air time were learning through baseball that they had underestimated its value. They found this out shortly after the Cubs introduced Ladies' Day to Chicago. Although it had been announced in the newspapers, not many took immediate advantage of the chance to see a game on the house.

One day, just before signing off, Pat Flanagan said over station WBBN, "Tuesday is Ladies' Day. Any lady who comes to Wrigley Field then will get into the game free."

On the following Tuesday, about twenty thousand women flocked to the ball park. Later, when the rest of us also announced Ladies' Day in advance, the gates were stormed by freeloading females, who filled the place on several occasions.

All of which opened the eyes of the advertising brass. Our experience proved that, contrary to general opinion, women didn't necessarily go out after lunch. Thousands of them stayed home and listened to the radio, creating a vast market which had been practically ignored. If, reasoned the brains of the industry, so many women would listen to baseball, primarily of interest to men, how many more would listen to programs especially tailored for them?

That was how soap operas were born. Some of the stations, instead of selling the whole afternoon to one sponsor, broke the time up into half-hour and quarter-hour periods and sold it piecemeal. Heart-tugging serials like "Ma Perkins" and

"Young Doctor Malone" poured out of radio speakers. The shows became so popular that they were used to fill morning as well as afternoon hours, and soon the nation's women were off on a gigantic crying jag.

It didn't happen overnight, of course, but eventually several sponsors pulled out of the Chicago ball parks to put their money into soap operas. At this point, General Mills, makers of Wheaties, moved in. The Wheaties people bought up all the afternoon time it could get, and used it to sponsor not only baseball, but other sports too. Within a few years, Wheaties did almost all of the big league broadcasts, and the "Breakfast of Champions" became a household phrase.

It was through Wheaties that I left Chicago. One day in the winter of 1938, I had a phone call from a company representative.

"Russ," he said, "we're opening a new territory in Charlotte, North Carolina. We'll broadcast Washington Senators' games from there by telegraphic re-creation and need an experienced man to do the job. Are you interested?"

I wasn't very much at first, but when he mentioned the salary, I caught fire. Suddenly, the idea of re-creating 154 major league ball games a year from a minor league city sounded just dandy, particularly when I thought about the darkening picture in Chicago. The ax had already begun to fall on radio row. Stations were pulling out of the two ball parks, and mine might be next. I might be in a minor league town, but I'd still be broadcasting major league games, for which I'd collect a major league paycheck.

So I went to Charlotte and re-created ball games for four years. I described the mannerisms of the Senators and their rivals without ever seeing them play. Every hitter stepped in and out of the batter's box between pitches, rubbed dirt on his hands, tugged at his cap, pumped his bat, looked at the third base coach to find out whether he should hit or take a pitch, and belted harsh foul balls into stands where fans scrambled for the ball. The pitchers all leaned forward for their signs, nodded their heads, took deep breaths, kicked at the rubber, hitched up their pants, wiped the sweat off their brows, and glanced around the infield before going into their windups.

I resigned myself to a life of making long stories out of short symbols, and got heartily sick of using my imagination instead of my eyes. I longed for the sights and sounds and smells and excitement and fresh air of a real, live ball park.

Sometimes I imagined that I was broadcasting from a radio booth in New York's Polo Grounds instead of from a studio in Charlotte. I talked about the Senators, and dreamed about the Giants. Mel Ott replaced Edd Roush as my special hero, and when he became the Giants' manager in 1942, I nursed fierce hopes that he could lead them to glory. He never did, of course, but I never stopped hoping. Show me the Giants' fan who did and I'll show you a traitor not worthy of the name.

At the end of the 1942 season, the Senators took me back into the major leagues. They invited me to Washington to work on baseball with the late Arch McDonald, under the sponsorship of Wheaties. The deal also included broadcasting Washington Redskins' football games.

Washington suited me fine. I liked the city, the people, the sportswriters, my associates at station WOL, and everyone connected with the Senators and the Redskins. I bought a house in Bethesda, Maryland, and could support my family very nicely on what I was making. My daughter, Judy, was born just before we went to Washington, and we all looked forward to staying there indefinitely.

I worked there for three years. Then one day, soon after the 1945 season ended, Jack Slocum phoned me at the station and asked me to meet him for a drink. I thought it was purely a social call. Everybody in our business knew Jack. He had been a familiar figure around big league press boxes and radio booths when he worked in the news department of the Columbia Broadcasting System. Now, he was radio and television director of the New York Yankees. His boss was Larry MacPhail, the same man who had once forced me out of baseball in Cincinnati.

"We're changing our radio setup," Slocum told me. "Instead of doing just home games and splitting Mel Allen with the Giants, the way we used to, we're hiring him on a full-time basis. We'll broadcast by telegraphic re-creation when the team is on the road. We need a second man to work with him. Do you want to be considered for the job?"

Did I want to be considered for the job? Did I want to work with the best announcer and one of the nicest guys in radio? Did I want a crack at the New York market, where the big network shows originated and where sponsors looked first for talent? Did I want a shot at national recognition? And did I want to be as close to the Giants as the ball park across the river?

Of course I did. But I figured it was a hopeless case. Larry MacPhail would never hire me.

"I'm pretty well fixed here," I said. When I told Slocum how much I was making, he said, "We can't match that, Russ, but that shouldn't make any difference. There's so much radio money kicking around New York that the guy working with Mel Allen will get more outside work than he can handle."

We chatted for a couple of hours. Slocum told me frankly that he was going to interview other announcers, but that I would have as good a chance as anyone. Naturally, I ended up by telling him I'd take the job if it were offered to me.

That was the last I saw or heard from Jack Slocum for a long time. As the days and weeks and months went by without a word from him or anyone else in the Yankee organization, I decided they didn't want me and that I was crazy to want them. MacPhail didn't like me, and he could have his lousy little number two radio job. I was happy in Washington. What ever gave me the idea that I wanted to leave?

One cold winter morning, I was awakened from a sound sleep by the jangling of the telephone. I grunted a weary "Hello," and a gruff voice barked, "This is Colonel Larry Mac-Phail. Do you want to come up here to New York and work for the Yankees?"

It sounded like a gag. We had a few practical jokers around town capable of pulling one like that.

"I'm Grandma Schultz," I growled. "Go jump in the Potomac."

I slammed the receiver down and rolled over. Two minutes later, the phone rang again.

"Listen," the same voice yelled, "this really is Colonel Mac-Phail, and don't hang up on me again. Do you want the job or don't you?"

This time I was convinced, and, after hastily apologizing, I agreed to go to New York for meetings with MacPhail and Mel Allen, who was in the process of getting his Army discharge. I had run into Mel occasionally, but didn't know him very well.

I didn't see much of MacPhail. Jack Slocum took me into his office long enough for a handshake, and then we met Allen at Toots Shor's. Still in his Army uniform, he grinned a greeting, and I knew we were going to get along fine.

When it was time for me to make an airplane back to Washington, we got into Allen's ancient convertible and, with Slocum at the wheel, drove to the old airlines terminal on Forty-second Street.

"Wish I could stick around a little longer," I said, as I climbed out of the car.

"So do I," Allen said.

"It's just as well you don't," Slocum said. "We'd never get to bed."

Then he and Allen drove off, and I made my way into the terminal building. I must have looked pretty awful because a very nice young lady behind the desk said, "I think you'd better walk around the block a couple of times before you get into the limousine."

I said, from force of habit, since I'd been saying it all night, "Whatever you say, Mel." When I got back, she said, a bit doubtfully, "I *guess* you're all right. Nobody will notice you if you don't say anything."

She needn't have worried. I fell asleep in the limousine and I fell asleep on the airplane. By the time we reached Washington, I was able to drive my own car home. And when I got there, I was too excited to sleep.

Not long after that, Merle Jones, the general manager of WOL, threw a farewell party for me, and invited all the Washington sports personalities with whom I'd been associated. Mel couldn't make it because he had just undergone a minor operation, but he gave a little talk over the telephone right from his hospital bed. He ended by saying, "Don't worry about your boy Hodges. We'll treat him all right in New York."

I was proud and happy and confident, and looking forward to my new job, but I got an attack of the jitters when it was time for me to do my first broadcast. Mel had gone to spring training at St. Petersburg, Florida, for two weeks, and I had to work alone on a telegraphic re-creation of an exhibition game. As I sat in a studio at WINS, New York, I thought, "New job, new studio, new market, new sponsors. The agency is tough, and suppose I blow a commercial or two. They'll have my head."

I'd been talking about Wheaties for so long that I was afraid I'd slip them in instead of Pabst Blue Ribbon Beer and White Owl Cigars, which sponsored the Yankees' games that year. The advertising agency, J. Walter Thompson, was efficient and businesslike, and they wouldn't stand for any serious bloops. I was still very poor on commercials, for I hated to read them, and I hadn't improved much from my Covington days.

I needn't have worried. I came out alive the first day, and felt better the second. From then on, I was all right.

Just before the regular season began, Larry MacPhail exploded a radio bombshell. Up to then, baseball announcers almost never went anywhere. They handled home games live and road games by wire, as I had in Washington. Now MacPhail arranged for Allen and me to travel with the Yankees, while the sponsors picked up the check. We would become the first to broadcast an entire season live.

Both of us were delighted. It not only made us feel a part of the ball club, but it eliminated those telegraphic recreations which annoyed me so much. I looked forward to the experience, even though it meant I couldn't take a regular evening sports show, which would have given me some additional income. But I knew I would gain more in prestige than I lost in immediate cash, and this would pay off in the long run, which was exactly what happened.

Mel Allen and I were inseparable. Both of us were hot fans, and we talked baseball by the hour. One night, shortly after opening day, he said, "You know, Russ, I've had a million thrills in this business, but there's one I missed. I've never handled a no-hitter. Have you?"

"I had two in Chicago, both by the White Sox," I said. "I saw Vern Kennedy throw one against Cleveland in 1935 and I saw Bill Dietrich's no-hitter against St. Louis in 1937. It's quite a thrill, all right."

"I sure hope I get one some day," he said.

About a week later, on April 30, Bob Feller faced us at Yankee Stadium. The way Mel and I worked, I did the fourth and seventh innings, and he did the others. I took over in the fourth, as usual, and he picked up the game in the fifth.

Feller was terrific. The Yankees couldn't touch the guy. By the end of the sixth inning, when it was time for me to work again, he had a no-hitter going, and it looked as if he were going to make it all the way.

As the seventh was about to begin, Allen, looking a little unhappy, wistfully started to turn the microphone over to me.

"You keep it, Mel," I said. "I've been through a couple of these before."

He nodded and grinned, then finished the game, which indeed turned out to be a no-hitter for Feller. That night, Allen ran into the late Bill Corum, then the sports columnist of the New York *Journal-American*, and one of the most widely read sportswriters in the country.

"You finally saw a no-hitter, didn't you, Mel?" Corum said.

"I sure did," Mel said, "and I got a great kick out of it."

"I see you didn't even let Hodges get on the air," Corum said.

Allen told him why, and the next day I was amazed to read all about it in Corum's column.

"Welcome to town, Russ Hodges," the headline read, and the whole column was about my generosity. "Anyone who will do a thing like that," Corum wrote, "is a real champ."

It was a tremendous tribute which touched me deeply. It also meant money in my pocket. Sponsors, advertising men, and all the people who had anything to do with sports read Corum faithfully. Nobody had paid much attention to me up to that time. Broadcasters came and went, and I was just another outlander. But after Corum's piece appeared, I was accepted as part of the crowd, and contracts began coming my way. Before the year was over, I almost matched my Washington income.

The season of 1946 was a rough one for the Yankees. The boys hadn't regained their peacetime legs yet, and the club had managerial problems. Despite his fabulous record, Joe McCarthy didn't hit it off with the new owners, and MacPhail fired him near midseason. Bill Dickey became the manager, but didn't like the job and resigned in September. Johnny Neun came in to finish out the disappointing season.

The Boston Red Sox won the pennant going away, after piling up such a big lead in June that nobody could get close to them. The Yankees finished third, which was a disappointment to all their badly spoiled followers. Even by that time, they had won so many pennants that anything short of first place made the season a flop.

Things were different in 1947. Bucky Harris, who had worked in the front office the year before and wanted to stay there, was prevailed upon by MacPhail to take over as manager. The Yankees started slowly, but gathered momentum, and were in first place by early June.

When I started traveling with the team, I became much better acquainted with the ballplayers than I ever had before. I saw them not only at the ball park, but on trains and airplanes, in hotel lobbies and wherever else we all gathered.

Genius finds its own level, and I found mine one day in

the locker room. I had to go down there after every game, and was gratified to discover a couple of shower room singers of formidable proportions. Tommy Henrich was quite a tenor and Johnny Lindell had a fine bass voice. The two needed only my baritone to give them a little class.

We all had our own favorites. Neither of the others could touch me on "Danny Boy," and after a while they didn't even try. By trial and error, we found that we were at our best as a trio with "I Had a Dream, Dear, You Had One, Too." The big thing about that number was that we all knew the words, so nobody had to resort to any phony tum-de-tum-de-tum-de-ling to get by. When we sang "I Had a Dream, Dear, You Had One, Too," you couldn't tell the shower water from the tears.

Our finest moments came after the Yankees won a ball game. Our best songs were tear-jerkers, but Harris took a dim view of music in any form, no matter how sad, after a tough loss. We didn't feel much like singing then, anyhow. I didn't even feel like going into the locker room.

In early July, Joe Page, who was the year's best relief pitcher, saved a game for Allie Reynolds, and we sang "I Had a Dream, Dear, You Had One, Too," after it was over. The next day, Page pulled a game out for Frank Shea, and we sang it again. The day after that, Buck Newsom, who had just joined the club, won for us and we sang it a third time.

Day after day the Yankees won, and day after day, Henrich, Lindell, and Hodges gave sweet renditions of "I Had a Dream, Dear, You Had One, Too." This happened for three solid weeks, for we won nineteen straight games. When we lost one at last, we were so far ahead of the pack that nobody had a chance to catch us.

On the day the streak ended, I pussy-footed into the locker room, planning to get out of there as fast as I could. Henrich

and Lindell were both in the showers, which sounded wet
and businesslike, for neither one of them was singing. Just as
I started to leave, Harris said, "Where are you going, Russ?"

"Out," I said. "You guys don't want me around here."

"Stick around," Bucky said.

"What for?" I said.

"So you can sing 'I Had a Dream, Dear, You Had One,
Too,'" he said.

"After a losing ball game?" I said.

"You guys carried us for nineteen straight," he said. "You
can't quit now."

So when the others came out of their showers, we sang "I
Had a Dream, Dear, You Had One, Too," and we sang it
every day for the rest of the season. I squeezed that one almost as dry as "Danny Boy."

Some strange things happen in radio booths, and one of
the strangest took place one day about a year later, while
Allen was on the air. A guy telephoning his wife somehow
got hooked in on our circuit at just about the time our engineer happened to be out of the booth. Mel couldn't hear the
man talking, and the man didn't realize he was on the air.

The fellow was a baseball fan, and recognized Allen's
voice.

"Hey, Mel," he said, "get off the line."

Of course nothing happened.

"Didn't you hear me?" the man demanded. "This is a pri-
vate line. Get off it."

When he still got no reaction, the guy blew his stack and
started swearing. For about a minute, ears must have been
burning all over the place. The engineer finally got back and
hastily straightened things out.

The next thing I knew, I was busy explaining that the of-
fender wasn't me. A rumor had spread around town that I

had had a fight with Allen and was trying to get him off the air. It didn't die down until we left on our next road trip.

At the end of the 1948 season, George Weiss, who became general manager of the club after MacPhail sold out to Dan Topping, called me into his office.

"We like the job you're doing," he said, "and we're giving you a new three-year contract."

The contract, which I signed on the spot, was a beauty. It called for more money than I got in Washington. I was also doing college and pro football, and picking up a lot of work on the side, so my financial condition was very healthy indeed.

I walked out of Mr. Weiss' office at peace with the world. It looked as if I were going to be with the Yankees and Mel Allen for a long, long time.

Chapter 5

While I lived with the Yankees, I died with the Giants. You can't control your heart in love or baseball. The Giants had been my team for twenty years, and they were still my team. I didn't consider that disloyalty to the Yankees, either. The Giants couldn't hurt us, because they were in the other league. The only time they would ever play us with anything at stake would be in a World Series, and the chances of this happening in the foreseeable future were remote. The Giants hadn't won a pennant since 1937, and they were still floundering around in 1948. That's why I died with them.

Mel Ott resigned in midseason of 1948 after six and a half years of futility. Horace Stoneham, the Giants' owner, surprised the baseball world by giving the job to Leo Durocher. Not only did Durocher come directly from the hated Brooklyn Dodgers, but he was the only Giants' manager in modern times who had never had a previous connection with the club. The Stonehams were noted for their loyalty to their own people, or to people who used to be their own.

This loyalty extended even into the radio booth. The Giants' announcer in 1947 and 1948 was Frankie Frisch, who had starred for the club during the first eight years of his fabulous playing career. While I was perfectly happy with the Yankees, I envied Frisch. I didn't want him to drop dead or anything, but I wouldn't have minded swapping jobs with him.

Larry Bruff, assistant to Ben Few, the advertising manager of Liggett & Myers Tobacco Company, must have been reading my mind. Liggett & Myers, the makers of Chesterfield Cigarettes, sponsored the Giants' broadcasts. I didn't know it, but they had requested the privilege of naming their own announcer. The Giants were perfectly willing to let them do so, but Horace Stoneham insisted on the right of refusal, which the Chesterfield people gave him.

One day Bruff asked me to go down to see him. Unaware of all the wheels that were spinning within wheels, I assumed he had a program he wanted to discuss with me.

He didn't mess around. The minute I walked in, he said, "We've been listening to you a lot. We want a new announcer for the Giants next year. Are you interested?"

My impulse was to grab it before he changed his mind, but I didn't want to take a job away from Frisch, so I asked Bruff what was going to happen to him.

"Frankie's all right," he said. "He's going to be one of Durocher's coaches next year."

"Larry," I said, "there isn't anything in the world I'd rather do than broadcast Giants' games, but I just signed a three-year contract with the Yankees."

"When they hear you're going to be our number one man, they'll let you out of it," Bruff said. "They won't stand in your way."

"If they'll release me, I'll be delighted to work for the Giants," I said.

"What do you want for salary?" Bruff asked.

So we talked about money for a while, and had no trouble coming to an agreement. I didn't bargain very hard. I was so happy I would have settled for anything within reason. I agreed to a one-year contract at considerably more money than the Yankees were paying me. Bruff told me that as soon as everything was settled, they would hire a partner for me.

When I got ready to go, it was still hard to believe what had happened. Bruff walked me to the elevator, and just before it arrived I said, "Larry, is everything all set then?"

"Everything but the contract," he said. "And that shouldn't take too long. Just to be sure there aren't any hitches, don't say anything to the Yankees yet. You'll hear from me in plenty of time."

I thanked him and walked out. I was so tickled I nearly broke into song in the elevator, and I had to restrain myself from dancing on the sidewalk.

The Giants! I was the announcer for the Giants! As my pal Mel Allen would say, "How about that!"

I got together with Mel later in the day, and told him about it.

"Don't tell anyone else," he said.

"I'd like to tell everybody," I said.

"I don't blame you, Russ," he said. "It's a great opportunity, and you've got every right to be proud. But make sure you have that contract before you say anything."

"What can hold it up?" I said.

"Well," he said, "I don't know for sure, but I'll bet Horace Stoneham has to O.K. you. Do you know him?"

"I've never met him," I said.

"A wonderful guy," Mel said. "But I wouldn't be surprised if he'd rather be told privately who's working for him than read about it in somebody's column. If this gets out before he hears about it, he might not like it."

"Somebody must have told him," I said. "With so many involved—advertising agencies, sponsors, and people like that —it won't be a secret for long."

"Don't be too sure he's been told," Mel said. "And, for heaven's sake, don't let any rumors be traced back to you. Just sit tight and hope everything goes all right."

So I sat tight. In the meantime, I was busy with football. I did a college game over a national hookup every Saturday and on Sundays I handled the New York Yankees of the old All-America Conference. Most of the college and half of the pro games were out of town, so I was almost always away either part or all of the weekend.

A month went by, and I didn't hear a word from Larry Bruff. I was getting nervous, but Mel told me to relax as long as nothing appeared in the newspapers.

"Do you think Mr. Stoneham wants somebody connected with the Giants?" I said.

"Not necessarily," he said. "Just take it easy. It's the middle of the football season. They might want to wait until later to announce it."

But I couldn't take it easy. I studied every gossip column in New York, both on the sports pages and elsewhere, looking for the item I dreaded to see. I worried about what I missed when I was on the road. I had bad dreams. My face twitched. I wasn't fit to live with at home or to work with anywhere else. I felt like a guy with an ax at his neck.

It fell at last one November morning about three days before I was scheduled to go to Columbus for the Ohio State-Michigan football game. The very last item in Dan Parker's *Daily Mirror* sports column read: "Why did Horace Stoneham suddenly nix Russ Hodges as his announcer for next year?"

That did it. Now the Yankees knew what was going on, and they'd be upset that I hadn't told them anything. If I didn't make a move, I'd lose that job, too. Much as I wanted to work for the Giants, I had to get out from under. If Horace Stoneham had nixed me, I was dead anyhow.

Mad, frightened, and frustrated, I phoned Larry Bruff and said, "Look, that item in Parker's column could get me into a lot of trouble. I've got a nice three-year contract with the Yankees. I think I'll stay where I am."

Bruff made no attempt to talk me out of it. All he said was, "I'm sorry you feel that way about it, Russ."

I didn't have time to brood. That afternoon my little daughter, Judy, was rushed to the hospital for an emergency appendectomy. There was a threat of complications, and we sweated for two days before the doctor told us she was out of danger. By then it was time for me to fly to Columbus.

As always on football weekends, the place was a madhouse. I had a suite at the Deshler-Wallach (now the Deshler Hilton) Hotel, and after checking in, I went down to the lobby to see who was around. It was crawling with guys I knew, all trying to get rooms.

The first one I talked to said, "Gee, Russ, this is the worst I've ever seen. There isn't a hotel room in town."

"Don't you have one?" I asked.

"Nope," he said.

"Well, come in with me," I said. "I've got an extra bed you can have."

While he was getting his valise, I met another friend.

"I don't know what I'm going to do, Russ," he said. "Looks like I'll have to sleep in the street."

"No, you won't," I said. "I've got a suite. You can use the sofa in the drawing room."

A couple of old pals from Chicago drifted by. They didn't have rooms either, so I invited them up too. "We'll get a couple of cots," I said. I met more stranded friends, and told them to go on up, and pretty soon I had eighteen guys bunking in with me.

I never do much drinking when I've got to work the next day, but I couldn't be a watchdog for eighteen other fellows, and I didn't try. The stage was set for a big party, and we had a wowser. It lasted until about four in the morning, and the lullaby that put the boys to sleep was my hundredth rendition of "Danny Boy." I crawled into bed with no regrets. Judy was out of the woods and I was near the end of one of the roughest weeks of my life, so I figured I had a celebration coming to me.

I intended to sleep until about eight-thirty, because I like to get to the ball park early. But some maniac had left a call for six. That woke me up, and I never did get back to sleep. After tossing around for an hour or so, I climbed out of bed and took a shower. It did little good. Not having had a good night's sleep all week, I was exhausted. On top of that, the phone kept ringing and guys kept waking up and trooping in and out of the bathroom and making so much noise that I thought I'd go out of my mind if I didn't get out of there. Just as I was about to leave the phone rang. It was my wife.

"Russ," she said, "after the game get on down to see Pat as fast as you can. He just had his appendix out, too, and they're afraid of peritonitis."

"Oh, no," I groaned. I was beginning to know how Job must have felt.

My son was going to school in Kentucky. I had half a mind to forget the ball game, but it would have caused such an awful snarl I checked the school. They told me a few more hours wouldn't make that much difference, so I decided to do the broadcast.

At that point, I was so distraught and tired and scared, I'd have bitten off my grandmother's head if she called. Besides, time was getting short and I was in a hurry. I grabbed my briefcase and went about three steps when the phone rang again. I picked it up and yelled a nasty "Hello."

It was the long-distance operator, and before I could tell

her I didn't want to talk to anybody, a man said, "Russ Hodges?"

"Yeah," I grunted.

"This is Horace Stoneham."

I stiffened.

"I just want you to know that I thought you had spread the story around town that you were going to do our games," he said. "Well, now I've got all the facts, and I realize it's not true. If you want to come to work for the Giants, it's all right with me."

"Mr. Stoneham," I said, "I'm sick of you and sick of the Giants and sick of this whole so-and-so, so-and-so situation. You can take your Giants and—"

In not very nice terms, I told him exactly what he could do with them, and added some more choice suggestions as they occurred to me. I ended by saying that I was staying right with the Yankees. Then I slammed down the receiver and headed for the football stadium.

If I land in the lower depths after I've cashed in my chips —and I probably will—I imagine it will be just like the next twenty-four hours. I couldn't find a cab for half an hour, and when I finally did we got into such a traffic jam I would have been better off walking. I mislaid my ticket and spent fifteen precious minutes fishing in my pockets for it, then found it in my wallet. Once inside the ball park, I had a terrible time reaching the radio booth. Nearly eighty thousand people were at the game and most of them seemed to be in front of me. An usher wouldn't let me go up the nearest aisle, and I had to take one that was far out of the way. Instead of getting settled a couple of hours in advance to have plenty of time to study offensive and defensive formations and memorize the names and numbers of the players, I slid into my seat about fifteen minutes before the kickoff. I spent most of them catching my breath.

I got through the broadcast somehow, although it wasn't one of my better efforts. The game was very important, since it landed undefeated Michigan into the Rose Bowl, but you couldn't tell it by me. I talked with the enthusiasm of a haddock. All I could think of was Pat lying in a Kentucky hospital and how I was going to get to him later.

That wasn't easy. He was in Corbin, about a hundred miles from Lexington, and there was no regular airplane service into the place, although it had an airport. Before the game was over, somebody had arranged to get me on a seven-thirty flight from Columbus to Lexington. It was the only good break I got all day, because I didn't have to beat my brains out going from the stadium to the Columbus airport after the game.

In Lexington I chartered a plane to Corbin, and the pilot agreed to spend the night there so that he could take me back in the morning if Pat was out of danger. I still had hopes of getting back to New York in time to broadcast the Yankees-Cleveland Browns game the next afternoon. I could do it by making an early-morning flight from Lexington to Cincinnati and flying from there to New York.

We arrived in Corbin at one in the morning, and they let me see Pat when I got to the hospital. It was after midnight, so a new day had begun, and it started on a wonderful note.

"Your boy is going to be all right, Mr. Hodges," the doctor said. "He'll be here a while, but there's nothing to worry about."

Tears of relief streamed down my cheeks. The doctor gave me permission to drop by again at five in the morning so that I could make my New York connections. Then I went to a motel and flopped into bed. That gave me less than three hours sleep, but it was the most refreshing three hours I'd known all week.

I had a few things to think about on the way home. In four days both my kids had had almost identical operations and complications, and both were on the road to recovery. With those worries out of the way, I could mull over another which loomed larger and larger as I approached New York.

Not only had I blown a job I'd wanted for years, but my own job was in jeopardy. What would the Yankees say when they found out I'd been dickering with the Giants without telling them? Under the circumstances, they'd have every right to fire me, contract or no contract.

And what had I been thinking of when I blew my stack at Stoneham? He had made a mistake and was man enough to admit it, and all he got for his trouble was a stream of abuse. I might as well forget all about the Giants now. Stoneham wouldn't hire me after that performance of mine. And if the Yankees fired me, I'd be in a fine mess. Baseball announcing jobs weren't so easy to come by that I could afford to dump two out the window as though they were cigar coupons.

The plane landed at La Guardia and I had just enough time to reach Yankee Stadium before the kickoff. Jack Tanzer, who had become one of my closest friends in New York, was in the radio booth when I got there. A former statistician for the Giants, Jack was a radio advertising executive who had helped me a great deal and acted as my adviser and occasional agent. He still does.

Sure that he knew where I stood, I wanted badly to talk to him, but there wasn't time. I got on the air almost as soon as I arrived, and stayed on until the end of the first half.

Then we all got up and headed for the Stadium Club in back of the grandstand, where I intended to talk to Tanzer.

Right after I got inside, a plump man with a cherubic smile on his face came up to me and said, "I'm Horace Stoneham."

I grinned sheepishly, shook hands and said, "I guess you know who I am, and I'm a little ashamed of myself."

"Let's forget it," he said. "And let's get together as soon as we can and get our deal set."

"Thanks," I said. "I was going to fly back to Kentucky tomorrow to see my son—"

"Come in when you get back," Horace said.

If he hadn't turned away, I think I'd have thrown my arms around him and kissed him. In all my life I had never met a man I liked so much so quickly.

Before the half-time break was over, Tanzer filled me in on what had happened. Rumors had been floating around town for weeks that I had the Giants' job, but nobody had bothered to tell Stoneham. As a result, when he was asked about his 1949 radio plans, he kept saying they hadn't been completed yet. Nobody believed him, and one night in Toots Shor's a newspaperman pressed him on the subject.

"You mean to tell me you haven't hired Russ Hodges?" the writer said.

"That's right," Horace said.

"Well," the writer said, "I'll bet you ten to one Hodges is your announcer next year."

"You must know more about it than I do," Horace said.

He came to what seemed an obvious conclusion—that I'd started the rumors. Before the night was over, he told a few people that I definitely wouldn't be the Giants' announcer, and Dan Parker printed it in his column a day or two later.

The rest of the story sounds like the happy solution of a soap opera. Tanzer, with the help of others who knew the facts, convinced Stoneham that there had been a mistake. That was when Horace called me in Columbus. My reaction, which would have made most guys see red, merely puzzled him.

He called Tanzer, told him what I had done and said, "What's wrong with your friend Hodges? I thought he wanted this job."

"He's drooling for it," Jack said. When he told Stoneham about all my problems, Horace said, "No wonder he was upset. Tell him not to worry. We still want him."

I waltzed out of the Stadium Club on a pink cloud, and went back to the radio booth to broadcast the second half of the Yankees-Browns game. It must have sounded like the battle of the century, because I pulled out all the stops in describing it, thus wasting some of my best stuff on a routine game in a dying league. Then I went home.

I called Dan Topping the next morning, and we made a date to get together in the Yankees' offices later in the week. Then I went to the hospital to see Judy, who was getting along fine, and flew to Corbin to visit Pat. He, too, was making progress, and I returned home for the last act of *The Trials and Tribulations of Russell Patrick Hodges*.

The Yankees were wonderful about helping me complete the switch. Trevor Adams had succeeded Jack Slocum as the club's radio and TV director, and with the help of Mel Allen, he got the sponsors to approve my release from the three-year contract. Then Dan Topping phoned Stoneham and made a date for me to see him that afternoon.

"I'm going with you," Topping said. "I want to make sure you get off on the right foot."

I grinned. "Thanks, Dan," I said. "I appreciate it. And this time I'll try to behave."

We drove over to the Giants' office, where Horace was waiting for us. I still felt a little funny about my blowup and I said, "I'm glad to be aboard."

"And I'm glad to have you," he said.

Topping shook hands with us both.

"I just came along for the ride," he said. "I wanted to be sure you'll take good care of my boy."

Then he left.

Chub Feeney walked in, and Horace introduced us. "You fellows will be seeing a lot of each other," he said.

"Let me show you around," Chub said. "That'll give us a start."

"Good idea," Stoneham said. "And, Russ—"

"Yes, sir," I said.

"You might as well get used to us," he said. "You've got a job for life."

Chapter 6

All I knew about Leo Durocher was what I read in the news-papers. A battling, light-hitting, wise-cracking bantam-weight shortstop who played and managed as if his life depended on the outcome, he had always been a controver-sial figure. He had played for the Yankees, the Reds, and the Cardinals before landing in Brooklyn in 1938. A year later he became the Dodgers' playing manager, and when his active career was over a year or so after that, he transferred his fire from the ball field to the bench. Profane, tough, and competitive, but capable of great warmth, he was a genius at handling men. Even his enemies, of whom Leo had quite a collection, conceded that he was one of the greatest managers of all time.

He won the 1941 pennant at Brooklyn, and was either second or third in all but one of the rest of his eight full seasons as manager there. Suspended for the year by Com-missioner A. B. (Happy) Chandler, he sat out the 1947 season, while the late Burt Shotton, taking over for him, won the pennant. Shotton, a close friend of Branch Rickey, the Dodgers' president, became a farm club consultant after Leo returned to manage in 1948. It appeared to outsiders that Durocher would remain with the Dodgers indefinitely.

Horace Stoneham wasn't so sure. Stoneham had a deep personal affection for his own manager, Mel Ott, but realized it was time for the Giants to make a change. While Horace had never said so, those close to him felt that he wanted Durocher from the start, and probably thought that Rickey was willing to let him go. However, he couldn't ask for Durocher directly because Rickey might then decide to keep Leo, so Horace attacked the problem another way.

His chance came on an airplane to St. Louis for the 1948 All-Star Game when he ran into Frank Shaughnessy, then the president of the International League. Shaughnessy was a close friend of Rickey's.

"Frank," Stoneham said, "do you think Shotton might be available to manage the Giants?"

"I don't know," Shaughnessy said, "but I can ask Rickey. Do you want me to sound him out?"

Horace told him to go ahead. A few days later Shaughnessy brought word that Shotton wasn't available, but Rickey had another suggestion—would Leo Durocher do? Leo Durocher would do very nicely indeed. A meeting was held in New York at the office of Ford Frick, now the baseball commissioner but then president of the National League. By the time it was over, Durocher was the Giants' manager.

The Dodgers, off that day, were in Montreal for an exhibition game with their farm club there. Horace phoned Durocher, and Leo flew right back to New York. After he and Stoneham came to terms, it was agreed that the story would be released the next morning. Leo left to meet the Giants in Pittsburgh, while every precaution was taken to guard against a news leak.

But Garry Schumacher, the Giants' publicity director, who knew Leo well, was positive the story would seep out. To make sure he wouldn't be held responsible, Garry spent most of the night with Horace. Just as Schumacher expected, Bill Corum broke the news exclusively in the first edition of the *Journal-American*.

Corum never told anyone where he got the story, but some people think it came from Laraine Day, who was then

Durocher's wife. According to one report, she was listening to the Dodgers' game on the radio when Leo phoned and told her he was returning to New York to see Stoneham. As soon as she hung up, she is supposed to have turned the radio off with the comment, "What am I listening to this for?" Corum's tip could have come from her.

Schumacher believes otherwise. "We were never able to prove it," Garry says, "but I'm sure it was Leo himself who told Corum."

I met Leo for the first time on the day I arrived in Phoenix, Arizona, for spring training in 1949. I walked up to him, held out my hand, and said, "Hi, Leo, looking forward to a good year?"

Leo, who knew I had been with the Yankees for the previous three seasons, grabbed my hand and said, "Hello, busher, you finally made the big leagues, huh?"

He was friendly, but we didn't have much time to get acquainted. I spent just a few days in Arizona, then made the rounds of the other teams in the league. I hadn't seen more than one or two National League games a year since working in Chicago. By the time the 1949 season began, I was just beginning to learn who was who.

Nobody had to tell me about the Giants, of course, but, after talking to Durocher a couple of times, I knew there would soon be changes. Leo considered the club he had only a nucleus of the club he wanted. "This isn't my kind of team," he used to say. "We need more of my kind of ballplayers."

Leo's kind of ballplayers were fast, alert, and smart, able to force the opposition into mistakes and to take quick advantage of them. He didn't mind having one or two slow-footed sluggers, but he didn't want a whole team of them. The 1947 Giants had hit 221 home runs for a new big league record and finished fourth. The 1948 Giants had led the National League with 164 homers and finished fifth.

"Where did all the home runs get us?" Leo said. "Who wants a second division club that hits home runs? I want a winner. Sure, homers will never hurt you, but they don't win pennants all by themselves. You need fast guys who can hit and run, and we don't have enough of them."

We opened the season in Brooklyn with nine holdovers from the year before in the starting lineup—Johnny Mize at first, Bill Rigney at second, Buddy Kerr at short, Sid Gordon at third, Bobby Thomson, Willard Marshall, and Whitey Lockman in the outfield, Walker Cooper catching, and Larry Jansen pitching. The Dodgers murdered us, 10–3, before a sellout crowd while Leo, target of boos from the fans and abuse from his old ballplayers, squirmed and fumed on the bench.

Our club was built for power, not speed. Mize, Cooper, Marshall, and Gordon couldn't run and nobody in the infield moved fast enough to suit Durocher. The season progressed and the results were almost predictable—we would win on homers one day and be outrun and outsmarted the next.

What bothered Leo even more was the failure of sluggers to come through after he carefully maneuvered to get them up with men on bases. Time after time, a long hitter would come to bat in the clutch and pop up or hit into a double play, while Durocher seethed.

"We're too slow to go for one run," he said. "We have to go for the bundle. So we get everything all set up, and a big guy gets up there and dies on us. I'm sick of power guys who don't hit when I want them to. The sooner we get rid of them the better."

The first to leave was Walker Cooper. The big catcher had

had a knee operation during the winter, and he moved with the grace of a steam shovel. Worse, as far as Leo was concerned, he lost his touch at the plate. He hit into so many double plays that Durocher gave up on him before the season was two months old. The Giants traded him to the Reds for Ray Mueller, another catcher, but Mueller wasn't the man Durocher really wanted, either. He had his eye on Wes Westrum, who had been in the Giants' system for three years.

Westrum had started the 1949 season in Jersey City, where he set an International League season's record by hitting five grand-slam homers in only fifty-one games. He joined us in Cincinnati, and Leo put him right to work. But Westrum had a disappointing season, too, largely because of a broken hand, which he neglected to mention. Nobody else knew about it until it was practically healed, and by then he was the regular catcher.

Day after day, Leo tried to get the most out of what he had, while Stoneham and Chub Feeney tried to get him what he wanted.

"We need a whole new infield," Durocher said. "Those guys around second base are too slow, and the other two are worse. And nobody ever gets mad. I want guys who will fight for everything and won't let anybody get away with anything."

He fought for everything himself, but after a while his heart really wasn't in it. Durocher was at his best with a pennant contender, but he had no patience with a loser. The 1949 Giants were losers from June on, and Leo refused to live in the present with them. He was more interested in living in the future with the team he visualized.

Besides having exactly the kind of ball club he didn't want, Leo, with good reason, suffered from a persecution complex after an early-season incident which hurt him far more than people realized. One day, while on his way to the Polo Grounds clubhouse after a game with the Dodgers, he got into a hassle with a fan. It was played up in the papers far out of proportion to its importance.

I saw the whole thing from the radio booth, where I was sitting with Al Helfer, my broadcasting partner that year. As I was giving the windup of the game, I watched Durocher walking toward the locker room beyond center field. Frankie Frisch was beside him when the scuffle took place.

"There's a ruckus in center field," I said. "A young fellow just jumped on Leo Durocher's back. Leo's lost his cap—he's shaking the man off—now Frisch is over there—so is Freddy Fitzsimmons—Bill Rigney's coming up, too—they're hustling Durocher up the clubhouse steps and it's all over—nobody threw a punch, and nobody got hurt—"

Then I went back and finished up the windup before signing off.

Leo met me later to do some commentary on a Giants' documentary film which had been made in Phoenix, so we didn't go to Boston with the ball club. We took a later train, going right to the station from the studio, and arrived in Boston the next morning.

We were greeted with headlines that made Leo blanch. Every paper in Boston had him on page one.

"DUROCHER SUSPENDED AGAIN—"

In the cab to the Kenmore Hotel, Leo, lacing his speech with colorful invective, raged with justifiable indignation.

"What kind of a deal is the commissioner giving me now?" he said. "He got me for a whole year before, and now he's got me again. Why should I be suspended? What did I do?"

I kept quiet. I realized it was a bum rap, but there was no purpose in saying anything.

"Any other guy," Leo said. "If it happened to any other guy, nobody would have done a thing about it. But me—I'm that bum Leo Durocher. There's a fight? I started it. There's trouble? It's my fault. A guy jumps me? I hit him. They don't ask me what happened. They just take it for granted that I did something bad. Why don't they call me in and give me a chance to defend myself?"

He didn't stop talking all the way to the hotel. When we arrived, he called Stoneham, who told him to return to New York. The commissioner had ordered a hearing at his office in Cincinnati three days later.

So, through no fault of his own, Leo missed the whole Boston series and the first game of a series with the Pirates back at the Polo Grounds. Frisch ran the club while he was away, giving rise to rumors that he would become the Giants' manager permanently. The rumors were ridiculous. Stoneham was prepared to go right down the line for Leo.

Chandler lifted the suspension after reviewing the evidence, part of which was a column by Bill Corum, publishing my version of the affair almost exactly as I had given it over the air. The ballplayers greeted Leo's return with a typical victory. They whomped the Pirates, 11–4, on home runs by Mize, Gordon, and Thomson. They won five more games in a row and led the league in the last week of May, then folded.

A month later we were in fifth place, and that was where we stayed.

"That's about where we belong," Leo said. "We're not a solid ball club, and we won't be until we make some changes."

Late in the season, he brought up the first two Negroes the Giants had signed. Henry Thompson and Monte Irvin had played most of the season in Jersey City. Durocher liked Thompson immensely, and figured him in his 1950 plans.

Irvin, not quite ready for the majors yet, was less than a year away.

We had pitching problems that couldn't be solved overnight. Larry Jansen was our only reliable hurler, although Sheldon Jones, Dave Koslo, and Monte Kennedy could win on given days. Leo thought they'd all do better if the infield were plugged up. Rigney, hampered by injuries, had to have a replacement at second base, for he had slowed up considerably. Durocher had tried Jack (Lucky) Lohrke there, but he knew Lohrke wouldn't be the answer.

The team finished two games behind the fourth-place Braves and twenty-four behind the pennant-winning Dodgers. As soon as the season ended, Stoneham started shopping around for Leo's kind of ballplayers. The obvious place to look was Boston, where two were kicking around loose. They were Eddie Stanky and Alvin Dark.

Stanky, tough, hard-bitten, outspoken, and the fiercest competitor in baseball, was a carbon copy of Durocher himself. By battling for every advantage and refusing to accept defeat, he had long since learned to get maximum use out of minimum equipment. He overcame the handicap of a small frame and little natural ability, and transformed himself into an outstanding star.

He had played for Durocher in Brooklyn, where he sparked the Dodgers to their 1941 pennant. Later, Durocher said of him, "Stanky can't hit, can't run, can't throw, and can't field, but he's the best second baseman in the business."

When the Dodgers sold Stanky to the Braves for one hundred thousand dollars just before the 1948 season began, Branch Rickey told Louis Perini, the Boston owner, "We've just sold you a pennant." Stanky was bitter about the deal, and thought Durocher was responsible for it. He accused Leo of stabbing him in the back, and told a Boston writer, "I could hit just well enough, run just well enough, throw just well enough, and field just well enough to make Durocher look like a great manager."

He also made Rickey look like a great prophet, for he led the 1948 Braves to a pennant. But he and Manager Billy Southworth didn't see eye to eye, and it was no secret that the Braves were willing to send him elsewhere at the end of the 1949 season. And if he went, Dark was almost sure to go with him.

Dark was a young shortstop who had broken in with the Braves the same year Stanky came to them. The two not only worked closely together on the field, but became inseparable off it. To the casual observer, this appeared to be a thoroughly incongruous combination. Stanky, brash, confident, and brutally frank, said what he pleased when he pleased. Dark, shy, deeply religious, courteous and considerate, never spoke out of turn.

But the two had much in common. Beneath Dark's mild exterior beat a heart as competitive as Stanky's. Like Stanky, Dark couldn't stand losing. Like Stanky, he caught fire the moment he stepped on the field. Like Stanky, he was constantly figuring out ways to harass the opposition. Like Stanky, he never conceded anything. And, like Stanky, he refused to give up until the very last man was out.

This was a second-base combination made to order for Durocher. In return for it, the Giants were prepared to sacrifice plenty of power, and power was exactly what the Braves were seeking. The dickering between Stoneham and General Manager John Quinn of the Braves went on all through the autumn of 1949. One hitch was the Giants' refusal to give up Bobby Thomson, whom the Braves at first insisted on being included in the deal. Thomson had good power and could run. He figured so prominently in Durocher's plans for the future that Stoneham flatly refused to part with him.

The trade was finally completed at the winter meetings in New York in December, when the Braves agreed to settle for Willard Marshall instead of Thomson. The Giants got Stanky and Dark, and sent Marshall, Sid Gordon, Buddy Kerr, and a young pitcher named Sam Webb to Boston. All but Webb had been Giants' regulars in 1949.

It was a controversial deal. Many observers thought the Giants gave away too much power. Others wondered how Durocher and Stanky would get along. A few pointed out that Dark was notoriously scatter-armed. A good shortstop most of the time, he was quite capable of heaving the ball into the dugout while trying to throw a runner out at first.

One New York columnist wrote: "Let's face it. Neither team won a pennant with this deal."

Durocher disagreed. Stanky and Dark were his kind of ballplayers. Leo was sure they would set the Giants on the road to a pennant, if not in 1950, then certainly by 1951.

Chapter 7

After switching from the Yankees to the Giants, I began to broadcast Columbia University football games. Columbia and the Giants had several things in common, not the least of which was an occasional rise from the floor to score a stunning victory when least expected. Neither team did that in 1949, however. The Giants, still building for the future, at least finished fifth. Columbia would have finished in the Ivy League cellar if Harvard hadn't happened to be worse.

The Lions opened the season with victories over Amherst and Harvard, neither of which I saw since I was still busy with baseball. These triumphs might have given loyal Old Light Blues a glimmer of hope, but they were actually meaningless. Amherst was completely out of Columbia's class. Harvard had one of its poorest teams, winning only one game out of nine.

When I picked up Columbia for the Yale game, nobody was aware of the helplessness of the Lions. But Lou Little, a great coach with a marvelous ability to get good results out of skimpy material, had an unusually inept collection of football players. Their slips began showing as soon as they met fairly good competition, and that was all they saw after the Harvard game.

They didn't just lose—week after week they got absolutely clobbered. I still shudder when I think of some of the games I sat through. The scores of these Columbia beatings spoke for themselves—33-7 by Yale, 27-7 by Pennsylvania, 63-6 by Army, 54-0 by Cornell, 35-14 by Dartmouth.

When something like this happens to a team, it gets everyone down. I would broadcast a slaughter, then go down and commiserate with Little and his kids. I felt sorry for them, as well as the fans, for Columbia people take their football seriously. And when I read about some of the great games I was missing in other parts of the country, I felt sorry for myself.

I certainly had nothing to be sorry about. I had an ideal baseball job and plenty of outside work to go with it. I was making a name for myself, collecting fine paychecks and meeting wonderful people. Instead of feeling sorry for myself because I had to follow the fortunes of a team that consistently got its brains beaten out, I should have been thankful for what I had.

But as this horrible Columbia season progressed, everything got out of focus. I griped about the dullness of my Saturday afternoons, and audibly wished I could spend them doing something else. I needed a lesson in humility.

I got one, all right. It hit me like a sledgehammer, almost knocking me out of circulation altogether. One day I was grumbling about Columbia; the next I was praying the good Lord would let me get back up into a radio booth and tell the world about a football game—any football game.

One Saturday in late November of 1949, I went to Annapolis for the Columbia-Navy game. It was a bitter cold day, and snow started falling at half-time. It wasn't much of a contest. Navy scored early, then kept right on scoring. The Middies piled up five touchdowns and could have added more if they hadn't gotten down to their fourth and fifth teams. The final score was 34-0, the sixth bad beating in a row absorbed by Columbia.

I was very tired after the game, and didn't feel too chipper on the train back to New York. It snowed harder and harder, and by the time I arrived at Penn Station we were having a real blizzard. I was lucky to get home to Tuckahoe, where I lived at the time, because the trains had to stop running before the night was over. Cold, wet, and exhausted, I fell into bed as soon as I got undressed, and went right to sleep.

At about two in the morning I awoke thirsty, and got up for some water. I filled up the glass and brought it to my lips, but only a little water went down my throat. The rest slobbered down my neck and all over my pajamas. For a minute I thought I had tilted the glass too far, but then I looked in a mirror, and nearly fainted.

My first thought was that I had had a stroke. The entire right side of my face had actually collapsed. My eye drooped and so did my cheek, half my mouth, my nostril, everything from my chin to my temple that was movable. I looked like a "before and after" ad, with two faces, one side normal, the other falling away. I tried to close my right eye and, to my horror, found that I couldn't. Tears kept running from it down my sagging cheek.

I had no control of the nerves on that side of my face. I had seen and heard about stroke victims, and it looked as though I had just joined them. Shocked and scared at the apparition that stared back at me from the mirror, I felt utterly helpless.

Then I tried to speak, and nothing came out but a mumble. With only one side of my mouth working, the other, flaccid and soft, hung lax and useless as little driblets of saliva seeped from a lower lip which curled down toward my chin. I reached up and pushed it back into place, but it flopped down again as soon as I took my hand away. I tried to speak again, but the result was only a liquid caricature of my voice.

I thought of the Giants and the Yankees and the Sena-

tors and the Cubs and the White Sox and the Reds and all
the hundreds of games I had broadcast since my younger
days in Cincinnati, and wondered if I'd ever broadcast another. I thought of unhappy Columbia and undefeated
Michigan and the other football teams, big and little, good
and bad, whose fortunes I had followed and whose stories I
had told over the air. I thought of the Georgia Skillet-Lickers
and Ramblin' Red Foley and the hillbilly music my mother
so detested, and of those mornings in Covington when I
played it for the farmers of Ohio and Kentucky. Could I
ever run even a show like that again?

I thought of Fenton Pugh and his singing lessons, and of
doing my scales and mi-mi-mi-ing around the house, and
now I couldn't even hold my lips together to form an em. I
thought of the party in Columbus and of "Danny Boy," and
now I choked on the words. I thought of the Yankees' locker
room and of Johnny Lindell and Tommy Henrich and of a
nineteen-game winning streak and of "I Had a Dream,
Dear, You Had One, Too," and now I couldn't even say it,
much less sing it.

What had happened to me? And what would happen to
me? How could I do a broadcast? And if I didn't broadcast,
what could I do? What would I ever want to do? How could
I get along without a microphone in front of me, without
sports, without the Giants? If I couldn't keep on broadcasting—if I couldn't keep on doing the Giants' games—if I had
to try something else—how could I keep going?

I turned away from the mirror at last, and slowly went
back to bed. My first impulse had been to wake my wife
and have her call the doctor, but it was a terrible hour to
call anyone and the blizzard was at its height. I'd wait until
morning. By then, perhaps, this nightmare would be over.

I suppose I got some sleep, because I don't remember

everything that went through my head that night. All I know is most of the time I lay in cold fear. I wondered how a thirty-nine-year-old man who had never been sick could suddenly have a stroke. I was young and healthy and in the prime of life. Sure, maybe I had a bit too much flesh for my height, but I certainly wasn't unusually overweight. I was a butterball, not an elephant, and a recent physical examination had showed that my physical condition was excellent.

In the morning I felt worse, for now, added to the discomfort of half my face being twisted out of shape was a terrible pain under my right ear. I wondered if I had mastoid trouble—maybe I needed an operation.

I no longer tried to speak normally, but talked out of the left side of my mouth. It didn't sound like me, but at least I could make myself understood. I tried to phone the family doctor myself, but couldn't get through to him. The blizzard, which had stopped, had knocked out some telephone lines. Then I remembered that Dr. Harrison McLaughlin, a bone specialist at the Presbyterian Medical Center, lived only a couple of blocks away. He did the Giants' bone work. When he had time to go to the ball game, we sometimes drove in together.

I described all the symptoms, and he hurried right over. He showed alarm as soon as he looked at me, then tried to cover it up with a smile.

"What's the matter with me, doc?" I asked.

"We'll see if we can find out in a minute or two," he said.

After I led him into my den, he reached into his satchel, took out a sterile needle, and stabbed me in the cheek with it. When I yelled from the pain, his face relaxed into a real grin.

"What's so funny?" I said.

"It's not funny," he said. "I'm just relieved. When I first

looked at you I thought it was a stroke, but it wasn't. If you'd had one, you wouldn't have felt a thing."

"What is it?" I said.

"I'm not sure, but I think you've got something called Bell's palsy," he said. "I want you to see a nerve specialist down at the Center. I'll arrange an appointment for you this afternoon."

"What does it mean?" I said.

"Let the specialist tell you," he said.

"Is it serious?" I demanded. "Will I ever be able to talk straight again?"

"Relax, Russ," he said. "If it's what I think it is, you'll be all right."

It *was* Bell's palsy, which is caused by the pinching of a facial nerve, usually due to extreme cold. I must have picked it up at the football game in Annapolis. The doctor told me that, while I might always have a very slight facial deformity, there wouldn't be any other permanent damage.

"You need rest and deep heat," he said. "Go to a physiotherapist for the heat."

"When can I get back to work?" I said.

"In about six months," he said.

Later I told Dr. McLaughlin that six months was a ridiculously long time. Over a month of the baseball season would be gone by then.

"Can't you do something that will get me fixed up sooner?" I said.

"Now, Russ," he said, "this thing won't clear up overnight."

"I've got a Columbia game to do Saturday," I said.

"Forget it," he said. "Let somebody else go out in that cold."

So I missed Columbia's seventh straight loss. At least it wasn't a bad one. Brown beat the Lions by a 16–7 score. It was the first time an opponent had scored less than four touchdowns since the Harvard game.

The deep heat helped me no end, and relieved the pain under my ear. Soon Dr. McLaughlin taped up my bad side, pulling the skin back into position, and I could walk around without scaring little children. But I still didn't have much control of my facial muscles. That would take months.

I found out later that all sorts of rumors had spread around the sports crowd. Russ Hodges was bedridden after a stroke. Russ Hodges couldn't speak. Russ Hodges was in a wheelchair. Russ Hodges was dying. Russ Hodges would never work again and the Giants' job was up for grabs.

Somebody called Horace Stoneham and asked him what he was going to do for a radio announcer in 1950.

"I've already got one," he said. "Russ Hodges."

"What if he can't work?" the caller said.

"We'll let Russ decide that," Stoneham said. "He'll tell me if he can't work."

Thanks to Dr. McLaughlin's tape, I could broadcast a fight on television ten days after my attack. The tape enabled me to control the movements of my lips and my right eye, which had stopped tearing. I still couldn't close it, but it was much better than it had been.

But what I really needed was a long stretch of warm weather, and New York is no place for that in the wintertime. One day, Horace Stoneham called me and said, "Russ, do you think you're well enough to go to Sanford, Florida, and give a talk?"

The Giants, who had once trained in Sanford, were still using it for some of their minor league teams, and they also owned a hotel there. Horace suggested that once I got down there, I might as well stay. I got the message, so I gave up all my other winter commitments and took off. I spent the month of January in Florida and, except for the talk at Sanford, didn't do a bit of work.

I went fishing day after day, lying in the boat with my right side facing the sun, and once came back with enough to feed everyone in the hotel dining room. Each day I could feel things a little better. Someone from the Giants called me nearly every day. When I knew I'd be all right I told Stoneham so, and he announced that I would continue to do the Giants' broadcasts in 1950.

As I got ready to leave for Phoenix to meet the ball club at spring training, my face was nearly normal, but I didn't have full use of my lower lip, which still drooped on the right side. It affected my speech a little, especially when I tried to pronounce letters like b, f, m, p, and v, all of which require full or partial use of the lower lip. I worked on these letters, and was still at it when I began the long drive from Sanford to Phoenix. I made the trip alone.

I talked to myself all the way across the country. When I got sick of the sound of my own voice, I put on the radio and listened to somebody else's. During the four days I was on the road, I guess I heard every scrap of news and every popular song of the day. Sometimes I sang along myself just to see if I could do it.

I was driving across New Mexico one afternoon when a band concert came on. There were trombones and drums and bugles and fifes belting out the wonderful beat of martial music. Pretty soon the fifes took over, and I began whistling, "And the monkey wrapped his tail around the flagpole—" and I whistled all through the rest of the program.

Only when it was over did I realize what had happened. Whistling requires as much pressure on the lower lip as the upper. If I could whistle, I could say anything, and I hadn't whistled since I first got sick.

I pulled the car over to the side of the road, and started whistling again. I could feel my whole lower lip as I tootled a John Philip Sousa march. Aloud I said, "very," then "much," then "fife," then "baseball," then "perhaps." Over and over, I repeated words with the letters that I hadn't been able to pronounce properly since November, and over and over they came out right.

I started the car again and stepped on the gas and shouted into the wind, "I can whistle—I can talk—I can whistle—I can talk—" and after a while I had to slow down and stop again because the tears were running down my cheeks.

I whistled all the way to Phoenix. I was still whistling when I got there, and every so often I whistle to this day. Except for an almost imperceptible drawing-down of one side of my mouth, nobody would ever know I had had Bell's palsy.

And since that ghastly night when I woke up for the glass of water I couldn't drink, nobody has ever heard me gripe about my job.

Chapter 8

The easiest way I ever knew for a guy to get a punch in the nose was to call Leo Durocher "Lippy." He detested this nickname, which was pinned on him when he was a fast-talking, loudmouthed New York Yankee rookie in 1928. I've seen Leo go red reading it and square off to throw a punch hearing it. Ordinarily, if one of his ballplayers called him "Lippy," Leo would climb all over him.

He laughed at the name only once that I know of, and I was with him when it happened. It was shortly after I arrived at Phoenix after my Bell's palsy attack.

Durocher had been telling me about Henry Thompson, the young Negro who had looked so promising when he came to the Giants near the end of the 1949 season.

"Russ," Leo said, "I've seen polite guys who say 'please' and 'thank you,' and can't do enough to make you want to help them, but the politest kid I ever met is this boy Thompson. Any time he wants the slightest favor, he says, 'Mr. Leo, please, sir, do you mind if I do this?' or 'Mr. Leo, please, sir, is it all right if I do that?' He's always dressed nicely, and he's modest and unassuming. I want to tell you, he's just wonderful. I've never seen anyone show so much consideration and respect for his elders."

A couple of weeks later, when it began to look as if Thompson was really going to make the ball club, Leo came over to me in the lobby of the Adams Hotel, where we were staying, and said, "Let's walk up the street and have a malted."

So we had a malted, then took a walk around town. As we meandered along, we saw a group of girls and boys gathered around a young fellow who was obviously the center of attention. We thought we were sharply dressed, for we both wore brand new buckskin jackets, brightly colored, freshly-pressed slacks, and ten-gallon hats, but this guy put us to shame. He had on green slacks, a yellow jacket and buckskin shoes, and was smoking a big black cigar.

"Leo," I said, "isn't that Henry Thompson?"

Leo peered through the gathering twilight and said, "It sure is."

So, when we came abreast of the group, Leo, with exaggerated courtesy, said, "Why, good evening, Henry."

Thompson held out his cigar, flicked off the ash with his little finger, and said casually, "Hiya, Lippy."

Leo and I almost choked. And when we got out of earshot, he sputtered, "Well, Russ, you can't win 'em all."

It was that same spring that I first laid eyes on Sal Maglie. He and several other big league ballplayers had been suspended by Commissioner Happy Chandler for jumping to the outlaw Mexican League in 1946. In June of 1949, Chandler announced that these men could be reinstated on request, but Maglie didn't apply immediately. Instead, he went home to Niagara Falls and spent the summer sharpening up his curve ball and control in semi-pro ball.

In the spring of 1950, he was just another guy trying to make the ball club. One day he pitched a couple of innings against the Cleveland Indians in Tucson, and had a rough time because he didn't stand properly while trying to hold runners on base. The Mexican umpires had given him plenty of latitude, but the big league umpires were much stricter, with the result that he balked three times.

I was with Chub Feeney on the bus going back to Phoenix, and Maglie sat nearby.

"He may not be able to pitch," Chub said, "but I'll bet he could always make a living. He looks like the barber who shaved me this morning."

And that was how Maglie got the name, "The Barber."

By the time we broke camp, he still hadn't made much of an impression. Durocher used him in relief a few times after the season started, but hardly considered him indispensable. One day after the season opened, I happened to be sitting in at a meeting in Pittsburgh when Horace Stoneham, who had been trying to make a deal, got a phone call. Some names were tossed around, then Horace said, "Well, we might let him have the jumper." He meant Maglie. Whatever the proposed deal was, it fell through, and Maglie stayed with the Giants.

Durocher started him against the Reds in New York in late June, but he lasted only six innings in a losing ball game. After that, he went back to the bullpen, where he stayed for another month. One night in St. Louis, Durocher, desperate for pitchers, started him against the Cardinals, and that time Maglie was tremendous. He gave up only seven hits in eleven innings, and beat the Cardinals, 5–4. As we were getting ready to leave the Chase Hotel for our train that night, I bumped into Stan Musial in the lobby.

"Where have you been keeping that guy?" Musial said. "He's got the best curve ball I've ever seen."

Maglie's victory perked up the whole ball club. As we traveled east on the train, everyone felt better, and we all knew it was because of Sal. He got the supreme accolade from Eddie Brannick, our veteran traveling secretary, who paid homage to newcomers only when he thought they had earned it. It was Eddie's birthday, and most of the guys went to get their own slices of cake. But Brannick cut a big piece off for Maglie and brought it over himself.

Before the season was over, Sal was the talk of baseball. That St. Louis victory started him off to an eleven-game winning streak. During it, he pitched forty-five straight scoreless innings, coming within four outs of Carl Hubbell's National League record. He ended up winning eighteen and losing four, and it was a long time before anybody around the Polo Grounds talked again about trading him.

Despite his ferocious appearance, Maglie was a gentle soul. None of us ever saw him lose his temper, and the only time I ever heard of his being upset at anyone was when a college professor was quoted in a magazine piece as saying that nobody could make a baseball curve—that it was an optical illusion. This hit Sal where it hurt, for he was very proud of his curve.

"I wish that guy would come up here," he told Garry Schumacher. "I'd take him across the street, and stand him behind a tree. And if I didn't break one around the tree and hit him, I'd give him my next month's paycheck."

Maglie made life miserable for the Dodgers. In 1950 he beat them four times without a loss and won five out of six the next season. He didn't have a losing season against them in his first five years, beating them twenty-two times in twenty-eight games. Once in a while, Roy Campanella belted one of his pitches out of the park, but for every home run Maglie struck Campy out a dozen times. Outside of Carl Furillo and Peewee Reese, who hit him occasionally, none of the other Dodgers had much luck with Sal.

Sal gave Jackie Robinson a particularly hard time. Schumacher once told me he doubts if Robinson hit .200 against Maglie. One time in Brooklyn, with the Giants far ahead, Robinson came up with two out in the last of the ninth. As he stepped to the plate, he yelled, "Those sportswriters who call you a magician are right. You couldn't be anything else and get by with that junk you throw."

Maglie didn't say a word. Robinson bounced a dribbler to him on the second pitch. It was the easiest kind of a chance, and Sal didn't even bother to throw the ball to first. He ran over himself for an unassisted putout, then disdainfully flipped the ball back over his shoulder at the fuming Robinson.

That spring of 1950, I was a little apprehensive about how Durocher and Stanky would hit it off, but there was no reason to worry. I didn't know it, because I was in Florida at the time, but right after the trade was completed, Durocher phoned Stanky at his home in Fairhope, Alabama, welcoming him into the fold. Soon after that, Stanky wrote Durocher a letter, telling him he was glad to be back with his old boss. And when Stanky arrived at Phoenix, he walked into the clubhouse, found his locker, dropped his luggage in front of it, and ducked his head into Durocher's office.

"Hello, Skip," he said. "Let's go to work."

"Hello, Eddie," Durocher said. "It'll be a good year."

They shook hands and that was the end of their two-year feud.

Durocher knew he wouldn't have to light a fire under Stanky, but he wanted Dark to be more aggressive, so the first thing he did was make Alvin the team captain. Dark had never showed much in the way of leadership qualities in Boston, but he took the job seriously. Whenever there was a rhubarb involving any of the Giants, Alvin was always right in the middle of it.

And there were plenty of rhubarbs. The 1949 Giants had been a docile collection of ballplayers who could take a ball game or leave it alone. The only one who ever squawked about anything or got into any arguments was Leo himself. But in 1950, he had plenty of help.

The Phillies won the pennant that year, but not at the expense of the Giants. We were the only team to outplay them, winning twelve out of twenty-two games. Long before the season was over, there was a full-fledged feud going on between the two clubs. The man who started it was, naturally enough, Eddie Stanky.

Stanky had discovered one day in Boston that if he moved around at second base just as the pitcher was getting ready to throw the ball, it distracted the batter. The Braves kicked and the umpire told Eddie to stop. There was an argument, and later Ford Frick, then the league president, after reading the umpire's report, warned that Stanky would be thrown out of the game if he did it again.

Warnings were never enough for Stanky. He always required proof. With Durocher's blessing, he went after some in Philadelphia a few days later. Andy Seminick, the Phillies' catcher, a big, burly guy, came to the plate in a critical situation halfway through the game. Just as the pitcher came down from his stretch, Stanky began moving back and forth, waving his arms over his head at the same time. Sure enough, Umpire Lon Warneke threw him out of the game.

There was a terrible argument, with Durocher and Stanky crowding Warneke, and the rest of the Giants yelling at him from the field and the dugout. Warneke, of course, stuck by his guns. Eddie was out, and Durocher finally sent Bill Rigney out to play second base.

The Phillies were mad, and Seminick was fit to be tied. Eventually, he hit a double and Mike Goliat, who followed him, poked a single to right field. As Seminick went around third base, he gave Henry Thompson the elbow, knocking out three teeth and rendering Henry as cold as a clam, and Durocher had to take him out too.

The next time Seminick reached first base, Goliat followed with a routine grounder to short. Dark tossed the ball to Rigney for the third out. Rigney started walking away, but Seminick smashed right into him. Rig, tearing off his cap and his glasses, started throwing punches at the Philadelphia catcher, and the next thing we knew, the whole infield was alive with battling ballplayers. I don't think I ever saw a better free-for-all fight, and it took a squad of cops to break it up. Tookie Gilbert, our rookie first baseman, nearly ended up in the jug for pushing one of them out of his way.

During the last week of the season, the Phillies, who needed only one victory to clinch the pennant, came into New York for two doubleheaders in a row. We piled up a 7–0 lead in the first game, but Monte Kennedy came apart, and the Phillies tied it up in the eighth inning. With the score 7–7, in the last of the ninth and Don Mueller on second base, Henry Thompson singled to right. It looked as if Mueller would score easily, but Seminick planted himself in front of the plate, and the only way Mueller could have gotten by him was to run up his front and down his back. Mueller tried to slide, but Seminick simply stopped him, waited for the ball, and tagged him out.

With Durocher, Stanky, and Dark leading the way, the Giants, of course, made a big fuss, but it didn't do any good. With the game still tied up, it went into extra innings, and the Phillies didn't score in their half of the tenth.

In our half of the inning, Monte Irvin reached second base and Alvin Dark pushed a single to right field. Seminick moved down the third-base line a few feet, trying to guard the plate the same way he had against Mueller. But the 220-pound Irvin didn't bother to slide for the plate. He

[1] Russ in his New York days with his son, Pat, now 29, and daughter Judy, now 22.

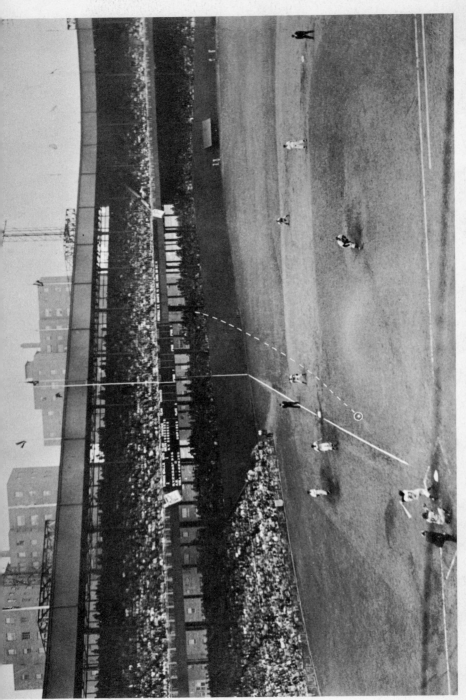

[2] Bobby Thomson hits The Home Run that clinched the 1951 pennant.

[3] Willie Mays making The Miracle Catch in the 1954 World Series opener.

[4] Willie Mays charging in to make a shoestring catch of a sinking liner hit by Gus Bell.

[5] *(left)* Willie Mays homers against Houston to put the Giants into a tie with the Dodgers for the 1962 pennant. *(center)* Dejected Houston outfielder, Jim Pendleton, looks toward home plate as fans depart with the souvenir home run ball. *(right)* Mays crosses the plate as teammates gather to congratulate him.

slid for Seminick, and when he hit him the result was one of the biggest explosions I've ever seen on the baseball diamond. Seminick went straight up in the air like a toy balloon. His mask went one way, his glove another, and the ball a third. By the time he came down, Irvin was across the plate with the winning run.

The Phillies never did clinch the pennant in the Polo Grounds. Jim Hearn shut them out, 5–0, in the second game of the doubleheader, and Sal Maglie and Sheldon Jones beat them by the identical scores of 3–1 in the two games the next day. The Phillies had to go to Brooklyn to win it on a home run by Dick Sisler on the last day of the season.

Now the Giants were Durocher's kind of ball club, a fighting, no-quarter-giving collection of wildcats who wouldn't stop at anything to win. This didn't mean that Leo himself sat back and let his ballplayers do the fighting. He was the same old Durocher, making a pest of himself with umpires, scrambling for a crumb that could lead to a victory, and putting himself in the middle of every scrap.

One day he got into an argument with the late Larry Goetz. He lost, of course, and finally called Goetz a nasty name. Goetz threw him out of the game.

The next day when Leo went up to home plate to present his lineup to the umpires, he turned to Goetz and said, "You remember what I said yesterday?"

"Yeah," Goetz said.

"Well, it still goes," Durocher said.

"You're out of the ball game," Goetz yelled.

If I'm not mistaken, that was the only time a manager ever got thrown out of a game that hadn't yet started.

One day there was an awful argument at the Polo Grounds after a close play at the plate in a game with the Pirates. Durocher and the late Billy Meyer, the Pittsburgh manager, screamed at each other like a couple of fishwives. Pretty soon Meyer, who had recovered from a heart attack only the previous winter, began to get red in the face. Clyde McCullough, the Pirates' catcher, pulled Leo aside and said, "Leo, go easy. This is an old man, and he's got a bad heart."

"Better him than me," Leo snarled. "I'm trying to win the ball game."

This was the man who had led the Giants out of the lethargy of 1949 into a third-place finish in 1950, only five games out of first place.

And this was the man who would lead them to glory in 1951, a year that every Giants' fan cherishes along with the years of his birth, his marriage, and the arrival of his children.

Chapter 9

While we suffered all the pangs of purgatory, the 1951 Giants, playing like Singer's Midgets, staggered off to a shaky start and then took a monumental nosedive. We opened in Boston, which usually has a sort of Indian winter in mid-April. The weather is beautiful until the baseball season begins, then it acts like March again. It doesn't snow, but it might as well. The wind howls, the temperature drops, and everyone sniffles and freezes and wishes he were somewhere else. With a little bit of luck, it might rain, and the ball game will be called off.

But when we arrived in town it was dry enough to play and damp enough to be uncomfortable. The Giants, chipper and confident after their driving finish in 1950, had looked so good in spring training that several observers picked them to win the pennant. Leo Durocher started the same team in Boston that he had finished with the year before—Monte Irvin at first, Eddie Stanky at second, Alvin Dark at short, Henry Thompson at third, Whitey Lockman in left, Bobby Thomson in center, Don Mueller in right, Wes Westrum catching, and a pitching staff led by Sal Maglie, Larry Jansen, and Jim Hearn.

My broadcasting partner that year was Ernie Harwell. On opening day he and I sat in a radio booth at Braves Field, shivering as the wind came whistling into our faces from across the Charles River.

"Bad enough we should play on a day like this," Ernie said. "Leave us hope that we win, at least."

Thanks to a fine pitching job by Jansen, who shut the Braves out, we did. That night, as we sat in the Kenmore Hotel lobby, Durocher cheerfully remarked, "We probably won't lost a ball game all year."

The next day that pipe dream vanished when the Braves beat us on a ninth-inning home run by Sam Jethroe. And the day after, our last in town, we really had to do penance. It was April 19, Patriots' Day, which is a legal holiday in Boston, and that meant a doubleheader in weather fit for down east hockey. The wind was worse than ever, the thermometer had dropped a few more degrees, and there was a strong smell of rain in the air. The trouble was, the rain stayed up in the clouds. If it had come pouring down, we all could have gone home.

On the way out to the ball park, Leo said, "This weather is murder for a pitcher. A guy could get a cold in his arm and be through for the year. I'm going to get ours out of here as fast as I can."

So after Hearn had won the first game, Leo sent all but six pitchers home on the five o'clock train to New York. The six were Monte Kennedy, Dave Koslo, George Spencer, Al Gettel, George Bamberger, and the veteran Jack Kramer. Before the second game was over, all six had pitched and Durocher could have used a couple more if they had been handy.

Kramer started one game all year, and that was it. Bamberger got into two games all year and that was one of them. As Durocher paraded pitcher after pitcher into the ball game, he kicked himself for leaving the club so shorthanded. When the game, an interminable affair that went ten innings and lasted three and a half hours, was finally won by the Braves, Leo was ready to jump into the Charles.

He and I played gin rummy on the train home, and neither of us said a word about the ball game. We were both thinking the same thing—that if he hadn't sent so many pitchers back to New York we might have won. But Durocher didn't need anybody to tell him that. All he needed was somebody to play gin rummy with.

That horrible ball game in Boston, which might as well have been played on the Dew Line, set us off on an eleven-game losing streak. Something was guaranteed to go wrong every day. The infield fell apart, the pitching staff folded, and the hitters died at the plate. We didn't have any luck either, for a losing team never gets any breaks.

A game against the Dodgers at Ebbets Field was typical. Hearn had a 3–2 lead in the last of the ninth, with two out, Duke Snider on first, and Jackie Robinson at bat. Robinson hit an easy two-hopper to short, and Dark grabbed it to shovel it to Stanky at second for a forceout—and the ball stuck in Alvin's glove. Then Campy hit one nine miles into the lower deck of the center-field stands, and that was the ball game.

We went down to the clubhouse, which was like a tomb. Durocher, sitting behind a desk in the visiting manager's office, was staring at his feet. He finally looked up, managed a sickly grin, and said, "Well—nobody ever called Dark glue-fingered before—"

Monte Irvin, normally an outfielder, had looked pretty good at first base in the last weeks of 1950, but now he was having a terrible time. He dropped an easy throw one day, and after that seemed to have lost his confidence. As the dark days of the losing streak went by, poor Monte went from bad to worse. He stopped fielding the ball and began trying to surround it, with disastrous results.

The losing streak finally ended, but Monte continued to flounder around at first base. One day I said, "Monte, how do you feel out there?"

"Like a bear trying to open a sardine can," he said.

Durocher relieved him at last. One day in St. Louis, he tossed a first baseman's glove at Whitey Lockman and said, "You're it." When I saw Lockman working out at first, I said, "Playing?"

"No," he said. "Working." He grinned, touched his front teeth with his fingers, and said, "I hope I keep these."

The move was an inspiration. Lockman, who had never played first base in his life, enjoyed seven fine years there.

"How did you know Lockman would be such a good first baseman?" I asked Durocher during a gin rummy game one day.

"Same way I knew Hodges would be," he said.

While managing the Dodgers, Durocher had shifted Gil Hodges from catcher to first base, where Hodges starred for years.

"Well, how did you know Hodges would be such a stick-out?" I said.

"Same way I knew Lockman would be," he said. Then, spreading out his cards, he added, "Gin."

Irvin went back to left field, where he regained his fielding touch in a familiar position. Things were looking up a little, but not enough. The Giants were fiddling around between fourth and fifth place, and they needed more than a new first baseman to get anywhere.

Bobby Thomson was a big disappointment. He went for days without getting the ball out of the infield, and by the third week of May was batting an anemic .229. Mueller was having even worse luck, for he was under .200.

"I get headaches from .200-hitting outfielders," Durocher

said one day during a gin rummy game. "We've got to do something."

I should have guessed what, but there are times when I can't see a bug on the end of my nose. Leo had been raving all spring about a 19-year-old rookie outfielder he had seen over in our minor league training base at Sanford, Florida. The youngster, playing on our Minneapolis farm club, was tearing the American Association apart, batting nearly .500 and making fabulous plays in the outfield. His name was Willie Mays.

We had swapped with the Yankees for spring training that year. They went to Phoenix and we took over their quarters in St. Petersburg. One day Stoneham and Durocher and a couple of others drove to Sanford to see Mays, and the kid put on a great show. He got two or three hits, including a tremendous home run, and made a couple of fine catches in the outfield.

At the time Leo said, "One year in the minors and he'll be ready to knock 'em dead up here."

Willie had been knocking 'em so dead in Minneapolis that the Giants hesitated to promote him because they didn't want to antagonize the fans there. But, with Thomson and Mueller not hitting and the club still in need of a lift at the plate, Durocher didn't care what would happen in Minneapolis. He went to Stoneham and asked for Willie on the spot.

Horace was just as eager to see Mays in a Giants' uniform as Durocher was. The Millers were in Sioux City for an exhibition game, and when the Giants phoned there, Willie was at a movie. Right in the middle of it, a sign flashed across the screen, saying: "Willie Mays. Call your hotel." Mays called, and that was how he found out the Giants wanted him.

He grabbed the first train east he could get, while the Giants, in an effort to ease the blow, took half-page ads in the Minneapolis papers to explain the situation.

I once asked Willie what the movie was.

"Russell," he said, "I was so excited I forgot. But I'm sure I must have seen it again later. I don't miss many of them."

He showed up at the Polo Grounds with six bats, a shaving kit, and a toothbrush, and, according to Garry Schumacher, the biggest grin in Manhattan. We were in Philadelphia, and the Giants got him on a train and sent him right down. The brass, including Stoneham, Feeney, Schumacher, and a few others, drove over that night to see Willie make his big-league debut.

I'll never forget his pre-game workout. Of course he was facing batting-practice pitching, but he belted it all over the place. He whistled line drives to all fields, and smashed screaming wallops into the upper deck of the left- and center-field stands. Then he went to the outfield, where he cut loose with that marvelous arm, winging the ball from deep in center to third base and to the plate without a hop.

As Durocher walked by Stoneham's box, Horace yelled, "Hey, Leo, how do you like him?"

"I'll marry him," Leo yelled back.

Willie's debut was hardly auspicious, for he didn't get a hit in five trips to the plate, although he made two fine catches. Durocher shifted the whole outfield around to make room for him. Thomson moved from center to left, Irvin from left to right, and Mueller was benched.

Mays went o for twelve in Philadelphia, and was pretty discouraged on the trip back to New York. He was really just a scared kid, and wasn't anywhere nearly as sure as Durocher that he could make it in the big leagues. Irvin sat with him on the train. He told me later he just tried to keep Willie's spirits up.

"Leo's right," Monte said. "He's going to be great. But right now he's just trying to get used to the idea of being in the big leagues."

The next day Willie smacked a home run off Warren Spahn of the Braves. I saw him after the game, and remarked it ought to make him feel better.

"Say, hey," Willie said, "it makes me feel a lot better, and I guess I'll be hitting a few more. But I still don't think I belong up here yet."

He used "Say, hey" when talking to practically everybody because he couldn't remember names. But he called Durocher "Skip" and Dark "Cap" right from the start. He calls Dark "Cap" to this day.

He went into another slump after the homer off Spahn, going fourteen more times in a row without a hit. He would have become discouraged except for Durocher, whom he worshiped, and with good reason. Leo treated him like a son.

Day after day during that first week or so when Willie wasn't hitting, Leo stopped at Mays' locker, put his arm around the youngster, and said, "Don't worry, Willie. If you go o for fifty, you're still my center fielder. You're the greatest, and don't you ever forget it."

After Mays got settled in a first-floor room in Mrs. Goosby's boarding house in Harlem, about six blocks from the Polo Grounds, Leo phoned him every day. He often picked Willie up there to take him to the ball park or to a banquet.

Willie was always doing one of two things when Durocher got there. If it hadn't yet gotten dark, he was playing stickball in the streets with a gang of kids. If it had, he was leaning out the window of his room talking to a crowd outside in the street.

One evening Leo drove his long sleek Cadillac up to Mrs. Goosby's to get Willie. Mays leaned out the window and yelled, "I'll be right out." Then, as the gang gathered around, Willie, instead of getting in beside Leo in the front seat, climbed into the back, leaned his head back, and said, "Drive on, chauffeur. Let's go."

It broke Leo up, just as everything Willie did broke him up. Mays was the only ballplayer I ever knew who could do no wrong in Durocher's eyes. Everyone else felt the lash of Leo's tongue sooner or later, but Willie never did. Durocher even got a kick out of his errors. One day at the Polo Grounds, somebody hit a routine fly ball to center field that a Little Leaguer could have caught, and Willie camped under it. The ball popped into his glove and then popped out again. I looked toward the Giants dugout, and Leo was laughing.

Later, while Chub Feeney, a Westchester neighbor of mine, was driving home with me, he said, "Russ, we saw something out there today that we've never seen before, and will probably never see again—Willie Mays dropping an easy fly ball."

I never did see it again, either. Mays has been charged with errors on fly balls that he had to run after and reach for, but never one that was right in his hands.

If Durocher was father to Mays when he first broke in, Monte Irvin was older brother. Nobody had to teach Willie anything about big-league behavior on the field, but Durocher wanted to be sure he would be a big leaguer off it, too. He assigned Irvin to room with Willie on the road, and he couldn't have made a better choice. Monte, mature and thoughtful, was a man of quiet dignity and great pride who realized at once that Mays, as a potential national figure, must also be a credit to his race. Willie was a decent youngster, but had had little formal education or training. Irvin helped to give the guileless youth from Alabama a measure of sophistication without robbing him of his refreshing effervescence. Under Monte's guidance, Mays learned to act with decorum and dress like a gentleman. Willie was devoted to him.

Willie pulled out of his paralyzing early slump with a triple and a single against the Pirates at the Polo Grounds one day, and from then on he was all right. Before he was through, he hit twenty home runs in 1951 and established himself as the most exciting center fielder in the business.

The Polo Grounds, with its huge expanse of outfield, was made to order for Mays. All he needed was roaming room, and he made some fantastic catches. Even more thrilling were his booming throws, which came in on a line from all corners of the field. He instinctively threw to the right base. Nobody ever had to tell him where the ball should go. Without ever having been taught, Willie knew better than anyone. Time and again, ballplayers have told me they could learn more about outfield play by watching Willie than by reading any textbook that was ever written on the subject.

As the 1951 season went into the summer months, the Dodgers piled up a formidable lead. But the Giants were moving up too. Maglie, Jansen, and Hearn were our solid pitchers, while Koslo came through occasionally. Spencer did a fine job in relief and so did Jones. We struggled up into second place in mid-June, slipped back a notch for a couple of weeks, then moved back into second place to stay for a while.

Durocher made his third major change of the year soon after the All-Star Game. He hadn't been too well satisfied with Henry Thompson's play at third base, and used both Rigney and Lohrke there from time to time. But these were only stopgap moves, for neither could handle the job every day.

"I've got to have a third baseman I can go with the rest

of the season," he said one day. "Otherwise we'll never win this thing."

At that point we were about ten games behind the Dodgers.

"Do you really think we've got a chance?" I asked.

"We *always* have a chance," he said.

When I asked Alvin Dark, who came from Louisiana, the same question, he replied with an old southern colloquialism. "Russell," he said, "if everybody stays well and the creeks don't run dry, we'll be there to take it all."

I'll be honest—I thought he was just whistling "Dixie" to keep his courage up. I had no idea he meant it.

Durocher solved the third-base problem with Bobby Thomson, who shifted to the position for a doubleheader with the Reds at the Polo Grounds on July 22. It was the first time I ever saw him play there, but I checked his record, and discovered that he had broken into baseball as a third baseman. He handled eight chances flawlessly in the first game and, although he made a couple of errors in the second, he seemed right at home.

He didn't return to the outfield for the rest of the season. Durocher alternated Mueller and Thompson, swinging Irvin back and forth between left and right, depending upon which of the others he used. Mueller always played right field and Thompson left.

Leo didn't fool around too much with his pitchers. In July we brought up Al Corwin from our Ottawa farm club. After using him once or twice in relief, Durocher began starting him, and Corwin did a fine job, but that was the only big change. Maglie, Jansen, and Hearn continued to start in their regular turns, with Koslo getting a shot here and there, and Jones and Spencer being used in relief.

Durocher kept insisting we had a chance, but it was hard

to believe. While we stayed in second place, we kept slip-
ping farther and farther behind the Dodgers. On August 11,
after losing to the Phillies, we trailed them by 13½ games.
To all intents and purposes, the pennant race seemed to be
over. With barely seven weeks to go, it appeared to be only
a question of how long before the Dodgers would clinch.

On August 12, with Maglie winning one game and Corwin
the other, we swept a doubleheader from the Phillies. On the
thirteenth, Jansen beat them again. Then Spencer in relief,
Hearn and Maglie whipped the Dodgers on successive days,
and we went to Philadelphia for a three-game series there.
We won them all.

Back at the Polo Grounds for a long home stand against
the western teams, we started by taking two in a row from
the Reds. Then Jones, who had beaten Cincinnati in relief,
pulled another one out two days later against the Cardinals.
We were supposed to play them again on Saturday the
twenty-fifth, but the game was rained out. The Cubs came in
for two doubleheaders in a row, one on Sunday, the other
on Monday, while the whole baseball world was suddenly
sitting up and taking notice. We had won twelve straight
and in two weeks had sliced six games off the Dodgers' lead.

In the first game of the Sunday doubleheader, Maglie went
all the way to the ninth before blowing a three-run lead.
Spencer relieved him and put out the Chicago fire, but the
Cubs had tied the score. Then, with two out in the last of the
ninth, Westrum belted one into the left-field stands and we
had our thirteenth in a row. Hearn beat the Cubs easily in
the second game, and that made it fourteen.

The Giants still weren't through. In Monday's opener, we
came from behind twice to win a twelve-inning thriller, with
Jansen going all the way. And in the second game, Corwin
threw a six-hitter for a 6–3 victory, giving us a sixteen-game

winning streak and leaving us only five games behind the Dodgers.

The best of things have to end sooner or later. The Pirates beat us on Tuesday and that finished our two and a half weeks in Valhalla. But now the Dodgers were running scared. Instead of accepting the pennant as their divine right, they knew they had a fight on their hands.

Durocher was like a raging tiger. Day after day, he swore and snarled and drove and fought, insulting the best out of his own men and the worst out of everyone else. He beat a path from the bench to the field as he battled umpires on every close decision that went against us. He hardly talked to newspapermen, who now mobbed him. When he and I played gin rummy—which was every day—each card was an enemy, each hand I won a disaster. There's always a lot of good-natured ribbing and kidding in a gin rummy game, and ordinarily Durocher's cracks were accompanied by a sly grin and a twinkle in his eyes, but now there were neither grins nor twinkles. He bit off his nasty remarks with real venom.

This was typical, for Durocher is one of the most complex characters I have ever known. Most managers are happy and at peace with the world when they're winning, grim and upset when they're losing. Leo was just the opposite. Give him a loser and he was completely relaxed. He would sit for hours after a game, calmly outlining his problems, showing why he lost, and explaining what he needed to win.

But give him a team with a chance to win and he was hardly fit to live with. He could see only one thing—the pennant. He wouldn't settle for anything less, wasn't interested in anything less, and wouldn't talk about anything less.

The closer we got to the Dodgers, the tougher Leo got. Back in August when we were far behind, he was fairly easy to get along with, and talked in terms of having a chance.

Now, with only five or six games separating us from first place, he jumped down every handy throat, and there was no question in his mind about the outcome. He smelled victory.

But we got on a treadmill after the winning streak ended, and it looked as if we might lose the pennant no matter what Leo thought. On September 20, after winning ten straight games in Cincinnati, we looked terrible losing a 3-1 game to Ken Raffensberger. He was a junk pitcher like Ed Lopat who, without throwing the ball very fast, could make it move around and make hitters break their backs trying to get a piece of it. The Dodgers won in St. Louis that day, so we were 4½ games behind them with only ten days to go. The boys looked so bedraggled and unhappy on the train back to New York that I felt like saying, "Fellows, you made a great race out of it and you've got nothing to be ashamed of. You're going to lose, but there's always next year."

Only Leo wouldn't let them get discouraged. He walked up and down the aisle of the car, saying over and over, "We're gonna win—we're gonna win—we're gonna win," and he had everyone else saying it before the night was over.

Only I didn't really believe it.

While the Giants were idle, the Phillies won in Brooklyn on the twenty-first, and the lead was cut to four games. They won again the next day while we were beating the Braves, and that made it three. We won and so did the Dodgers on the twenty-third, but we gained another half game on the twenty-fourth by beating the Braves while Brooklyn was idle.

Now we were two and a half games behind, with four games to play in six days. We all would have felt better if we could face the Dodgers again, but the season's series between the two teams was all over. We had to depend on the Phillies and the Braves to do the job for us.

On September 25, the Braves creamed the Dodgers twice
while Hearn beat the Phillies, and that pulled Brooklyn's
margin down to a single game. Jansen beat the Phillies again
the next day while the Dodgers were stopping the Braves,
leaving us still a game behind with only two left to play.

Now all we could do was sweat out two idle days, hoping
the Dodgers would lose. They finished their disastrous in-
vasion of Boston by getting whacked again on the twenty-
seventh, leaving themselves half a game in front. Then
they headed for Philadelphia for the three-game series that
would end their regular season. We went to Boston and spent
our second off-day, the twenty-eighth, listening to a fight
over the radio in the Kenmore Hotel dining room. Right in
the middle of it, Jimmy Powers interrupted his broadcast to
yell, "Andy Seminick just hit a home run and the Phillies
have beaten the Dodgers."

And that put the pennant race in a flat-footed tie, with
two games to go for each team.

On Saturday the twenty-ninth, Maglie whipped the
Braves, but the Dodgers won in Philadelphia, so it was still
all even. The next day it was so dark and the weather so
threatening in Boston that the game was advanced half an
hour to make sure it would be played. Jansen didn't waste
any time. He clicked off a 3–2 victory in two hours and one
minute, so we made the five o'clock train for New York with
no trouble at all.

In the meantime, things were moving much more slowly in
Philadelphia. The game not only started half an hour behind us, but the first five innings took forever. By the time
we climbed aboard the train, they were only in the seventh
inning, with the Dodgers trailing, 8–5.

It looked as if we were in.

Chapter 10

Just to make sure we wouldn't be caught short, plenty of champagne had been put aboard the train, so it could be quickly broken out the minute word came that we had won the pennant. The city of New York also had planned a reception for us on our arrival at Grand Central Station. If the Dodgers lost, nobody could say we weren't prepared for a victory celebration.

There was a telephone on the train. I grabbed it the minute I got aboard and called WMCA, our radio station in New York. They could get the game in Philadelphia, which we couldn't, so they began relaying the play-by-play to me, while the whole ball club gathered around.

"The Dodgers are up in their eighth . . ." I yelled.

"Still behind, 8–5?" somebody asked.

"Still behind, 8–5," I said.

"Only six outs to go—" someone began.

"Shut up!" Durocher roared. "You want to jinx us?"

"Pafko flied out," I yelled. "Hodges up."

I strained to hear, which wasn't easy. Telephones on trains were fairly new then, and the connection wasn't too good. Between that and the clattering of the wheels, I had quite a job.

Somebody started to speak, and I held up my hand.

"Quiet!" It was Leo again, and there was both volume and authority in his voice. The silence was instant, and I concentrated on the telephone.

"Hodges is on with an infield hit," I yelled. "Cox up . . .

Cox singles . . . that brings up Erskine . . . no, Walker's batting for him . . . *Walker doubles* . . . two runs in for the Dodgers . . ."

Somebody swore, and a couple of guys groaned.

"Now it's 8–7 . . . Thompson . . . Don Thompson running for Walker . . . wait a minute . . . the Phillies pulled Drews out of there . . . Roberts going in to pitch . . ."

"Good," said Leo.

"Furillo's the hitter," I yelled above the sound of the clacking train wheels.

"Get him!" Leo muttered.

"Ball . . . strike . . . *Furillo singles* . . . Thompson scores . . . that ties it up . . ."

"Oh, no—" it was Stanky's voice, and it trailed off in bitter anguish.

Roberts finally got out of the inning, but it was 8–8. The Phillies didn't score in their eighth, and it was still tied up in the ninth, so they went into extra innings. Neither team scored in the tenth or eleventh, and the Dodgers were blanked in their half of the twelfth.

"Who's the hitter?" somebody said.

"Roberts," I said. A couple of minutes later, I yelled, "Roberts walks . . . Pellagrini's up . . . he bunts . . . Newcombe grabs it and throws to second . . . *Roberts beats the throw . . . the Phillies have men on first and second with nobody out . . .*"

There was a quick cheer which died the minute I raised my hand. The brakes screeched and the train began to slow down. They were still screeching as we moved down the tracks in the darkness into Westerly.

"Now it's Ashburn . . ." I yelled. "He forces Pellagrini, but Roberts is on third . . . Jones walks . . . the Phillies have the bases loaded . . . one out . . . Ennis up."

"Will he yank Newcombe?" somebody asked.

"Not for Ennis," Durocher said. "Right-handed hitter—" his voice trailed off.

"Strike," I yelled. "Ball . . . foul . . . ball two . . . Ennis fans . . . it's Waitkus . . ."

"Left-handed hitter," somebody said.

"He'll leave him in," Leo said. He was right. Newcombe stayed in the ball game.

"Waitkus belts a low line drive to second," I yelled . . . "Oh—they say Robinson made a dive and a tremendous catch . . . the Phillies are arguing that he trapped the ball . . . the umpire says no . . . the Dodgers are out of the inning . . ."

Now the train was moving again, and the groan that went up almost drowned out the sound of the clacking wheels. Dark walked down the car, peered out a window, and walked back. Stanky kept shaking his head. Irvin pursed his lips and Mays' usual sunny grin was replaced by a deep frown.

The Dodgers failed to score in the thirteenth, and Newcombe got the first two Phillies out in the bottom of the inning. When he walked two men in a row, Manager Chuck Dressen took him out for Bud Podbielan, who got the side out.

Now it was Brooklyn's half of the fourteenth, and we wondered how much longer this could go on. It was pitch dark outside, and all I could see was the blinking of widely spaced lights as we roared through the Connecticut countryside.

"Robinson's up . . ."

"Get him out of there!" Leo grunted.

"He hits one . . . it's gone . . . left-center field stands . . . way up . . ." my voice dropped, and I suddenly felt as if a heavy weight had just fallen on my head. Then I said, "9–8, Dodgers . . ."

That was the way the game ended, and Eddie Brannick went up to the other end of the car to tell the porter to pack up the champagne. Instead of a party on the train that night, we faced the first of a three-game playoff series at Ebbets Field the next afternoon.

I thanked them at the radio station, then hung up and walked slowly through the car. Silent as death, the ballplayers found seats, and with shoulders hunched and heads down, sank into them.

"Hey," Stanky yelled, "we're still in this thing. We'll get 'em tomorrow."

"That's right," Dark yelled. "We haven't lost it."

"And we're not going to," Durocher yelled. "We've got 'em! We didn't come all this way to lose."

I got off the train in Stamford, and I heard later that about twenty-five hundred fans showed up at Grand Central to meet the team. They cheered, and Hilda Chester, the perennial Durocher fan, rang her cowbell, but it was hardly a celebration. As one player remarked to me later, "We all felt as if somebody started handing us ten thousand dollar bills and then pulled them away just as we reached."

The playoffs opened in Brooklyn the next day, with Jim Hearn facing Ralph Branca. Pafko hit a home run in the second to give the Dodgers an early lead, but Thomson smashed one with Irvin on base in the fourth, and, as it turned out, that was enough to win the ball game. Irvin's homer in the eighth gave us an insurance run, making the final score 3–1.

Everyone packed up and went across the river to the Polo Grounds for the last two games. The second was a nightmare for us. Jones, our starting pitcher, didn't last three innings, and Spencer and Corwin, who followed him, weren't any

better. It didn't matter. Clem Labine pitched a six-hit shutout, and the Dodgers won a 10–0 decision.

So now we were down to one game, and I went to the ball
park feeling terrible. Between the lousy weather in Boston,
my screaming over the sound of the train wheels, not enough
sleep, and the excitement of the past few days, I had killed
all my resistance and acquired a wicked cold. I was up gar-
gling most of the night, and just to make sure I hadn't lost
my voice, I kept talking into an imaginary microphone at
home, which only made my throat worse. I had trouble
breathing, my nose was running, and I was sure I had a fever,
but I didn't dare try to find out. I wouldn't even look at a
thermometer, much less put one in my mouth.

Ernie Harwell met me at the Polo Grounds, and we went
upstairs to check everything in the radio and television
booths. He would start and finish with TV and I with radio.
We still had a couple of hours before the ball game, but I
liked to get going early on an important broadcast. I looked
around the radio booth, and everything seemed all right. Bob
Prince, the Pittsburgh announcer, was in town with Ralph
Kiner, then the National League home run king. We had invited them to sit with us, and there was plenty of room.

The radio station phoned to tell me a frantic call had come
in from station KMOX in St. Louis. They wanted to carry
the game and could we set Harry Caray up in a booth? We
couldn't, because the Dodgers had the visitors' booth, and
we were using the spare booth for television. I told them not
to worry—we'd do something. We ended up putting Caray
in the same booth with us, and hanging a blanket between
his microphone and ours. We could still squeeze Prince and
Kiner in, which made things pretty chummy, but at least
everybody could see the ball game.

As I sat down for the broadcast, I felt a little like the days in Chicago, when a whole string of announcers kept yelling into each other's ears. Caray isn't exactly a shrinking violet behind the microphone and neither am I, so the odds were in favor of confusion.

The crowd was big, but far from a sellout. The Polo Grounds capacity of fifty-six thousand was hardly taxed by the thirty-four thousand who showed up, but I guess a lot of people figured the Giants didn't have a chance after that 10–0 debacle the day before. In the years since, I've run into about a million who claim they saw the ball game. Maybe they were there in spirit.

Both managers went with their best—Maglie for us and Newcombe for them. The Dodgers scored in the first inning on two walks and Jackie Robinson's single, but we tied it up in the seventh on Irvin's double, Lockman's sacrifice, and Thomson's outfield fly. That was Bobby's ninety-seventh run batted in of the season.

So the score stood 1–1 when the Dodgers came up for their half of the eighth. By that time, the crowd was in such an uproar and I was so excited that I almost forgot my sore throat. We were approaching what the boys in the back room like to refer to as the moment of truth. And, no matter what happened, the noise was deafening, for the crowd's loyalties were sharply divided. About half the people in the ball park were Giants' fans and the other half were for the Dodgers.

Maglie got Furillo, who led off for Brooklyn in the eighth, but Reese singled and went to third on Snider's hit. Then poor Maglie, who had thrown only three wild pitches all season, picked that moment to throw another, and in came Reese with the tie-breaking run. Robinson walked, then Snider scored on Pafko's hit. Before the inning was over, the Dodgers picked up a third run on Cox's single, and Brooklyn had a 4–1 lead.

I kept on talking, but my heart wasn't in it. The Giants didn't score in the eighth, when Maglie went out for a pinch-hitter, and it didn't look as if we'd do much better in the ninth. Newcombe, who had allowed only four hits in eight innings, seemed to be getting stronger instead of weaker.

Down in the Giants' dugout, everybody was crouching on the steps, while Leo walked up and down, clapping his hands and kicking up dirt in the third-base coach's box. Alvin Dark, the lead-off batter, stood swinging his black bat as he watched Newcombe heat up. Don Mueller, who followed him, was swinging a couple of bats behind him.

I looked at those guys, and thought, "Maybe they can do something—" but I wasn't too hopeful.

I should have known better. Dark beat out an infield hit and Mueller sent him to third with a shot into right field. Half the crowd was yelling and the other half was still as Monte Irvin came up. When he popped up for the first out, the crowd noises reversed. I could hear Caray on the other side of the blanket telling his St. Louis fans what was going on, while I tried not to sound like a funeral director as I talked into my own microphone.

Whitey Lockman was up, and the Giants' fans started cheering and clapping again. It all dissolved into a roar as Lockman, a notorious bad-ball hitter, rammed a pitch that was high and maybe six inches outside into the left field corner for a double, scoring Dark and sending Mueller to third.

Now the joint was really coming apart. Everybody in it was either yelling for the Giants to keep going or for the Dodgers to stop them and in all the confusion nobody noticed that Mueller was hurt. He had sprained his ankle sliding into third base. Durocher and Larry Goetz, the third-base umpire, were bending over him, while Doc Bowman, our trainer, was hurrying out from the dugout. After a few minutes' delay, Mueller had to be carried off the field, and Clint Hartung went in to run for him.

Bobby Thomson was up next, but there was another delay, for, just as he stepped into the batter's box, Chuck Dressen, the Dodgers' manager, walked out to the mound. He and Reese and Robinson and Rube Walker, the catcher, all stood around talking to Newcombe, and finally Dressen waved to the bullpen. While the roars of the crowd came in great waves as Giants' and Dodgers' fans alike indulged in a cacophony of shrieks, Ralph Branca started coming in to pitch for the Dodgers.

He took his warmups while Thomson, standing between the on-deck circle and the batter's box, watched him, his eyes following the ball as it went back and forth between Branca and Walker. Hartung was doing knee bends on third base, while Lockman stood with his hands on his hips at second.

Finally Branca nodded that he was ready, and, as Thomson moved toward the plate, the thought flashed through my mind that Branca might have orders to pass him and fill the bases, but that would put the winning run on base and bring up Willie Mays, so I dismissed the idea.

I don't remember exactly what I said into the microphone, and the station didn't put it on tape, but there's a fellow on Twelfth Street in Brooklyn named Lawrence Goldberg to whom I am forever indebted. Mr. Goldberg was listening to the game, and had a little home recorder hooked up to his radio. The next day, he called and said, "I want you to have this tape," and it turned out to be the only one in existence. It's been copied hundreds of times, and whenever I feel down or blue, I turn it on. It perks me right up, for it brings back the greatest thrill of my broadcasting career.

[6] Russ *(left)* and his San Francisco broadcasting partner, Lon Simmons.

[7] Willie Mays and Giants' coach Whitey Lockman in a heated discussion with Umpire Jocko Conlan at Los Angeles. They lost the argument.

WIDE WORLD PHOTOS

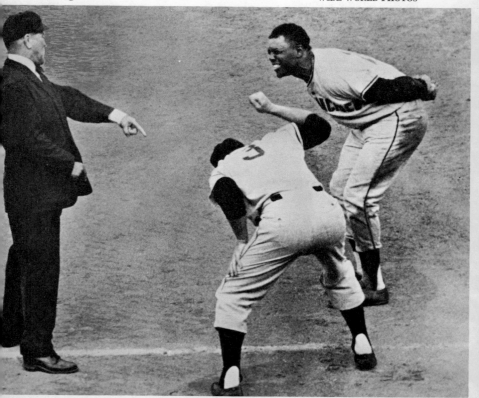

[8] Dick LeMay gives Harvey Kuenn a champagne bath after the Giants win the playoffs in Los Angeles.

[9] More than fifty thousand milling, cheering people jam the International Airport in San Francisco to greet the returning heroes.

[10] Mays steals second in the '62 World Series.

[11] No need to ask why the sixth game of the '62 Series had to be postponed.

[12] Right fielder Felipe Alou leaps high for Roger Maris' long drive in the first Series game, but the ball hits the fence and bounces back into play, scoring Tom Tresh and Bobby Richardson.

The first part is pretty clear in my mind. Here's how it went:

"So don't go away . . . light up that Chesterfield . . . stay right with us and we'll see how Ralph Branca will fare against Bobby Thomson . . . Thomson against the Brooklyn club has hit a lot of long ones this year . . . he has seven home runs . . .

"Thomson is on the biggest spot of his entire career . . . he'll be up there against Branca, swinging . . . a home run would win it and win the championship . . . a single to the outfield would more than likely tie up the ball game and keep the inning going . . . Leo Durocher runs over and talks to Bobby . . . Branca's on the spot . . . he knows it . . . the big boy from Mount Vernon, New York, with a slight cold, wipes the perspiration from his brow . . . and the Dodgers play their infield deep . . . there's no double-play possibility on a ground ball . . . Billy Cox is deep . . ."

I remember that my throat hurt and my voice was hoarse and that I fought to keep talking without making it sound as if every word would be my last. I remember looking at the base runners and noticing that neither was taking a very long lead. Hartung was only a few steps off third and Lockman very close to second.

I remember saying: "Branca pitches . . . and Bobby Thomson takes a strike called, on the inside corner . . . Branca throws again . . . there's a long fly . . ."

I remember stretching my neck, trying to follow the flight of the ball, and I remember the great roar that turned the Polo Grounds into a madhouse and I remember screaming into the microphone. But if it hadn't been for Mr. Goldberg's tape recorder, I wouldn't have the slightest idea what I said. It was this:

". . . it's gonna be . . . I believe . . . *the Giants win the*

*pennant . . . the Giants win the pennant . . . the Giants win
the pennant . . . the Giants win the pennant . . . Bobby hit
it into the lower deck of the left-field stands . . . the Giants
win the pennant and they're going crazy . . . I don't believe
it . . . I don't believe it . . . I will not believe it . . . Bobby
Thomson hit a line drive into the lower deck of the left-field
stands and the place is going crazy . . . the Giants—Horace
Stoneham's got a winner . . . and they're picking up Bobby
Thomson and carrying him off the field . . . the Giants just
won a pennant . . ."*

The whole wild scene came back to me later in little epi-
sodes . . . Thomson rounding first base, then leaping fifteen
feet into the air when he saw that the ball was gone . . .
Hartung jumping up and down on the plate, and Lockman
doing the same thing as he scored . . . Stanky galloping out
from the dugout, hauling Durocher down with a flying tackle
and holding him in an insane, happy bear hug . . . the marvelous grin on Bobby Thomson's long face as he rounded
third base and headed for the plate . . .

And the most vivid memory of all and the most poignant
—Jackie Robinson standing near second base, watching
Thomson to make sure he touched every base. Only after
Bobby crossed the plate did Robinson turn and slowly start
walking to the clubhouse behind center field.

I had to get to the locker room too, but I couldn't leave a
live microphone untended. Ernie had already left the television booth and started through the jumping, howling crowd
to reach the field and head for the clubhouse. Harry Caray
was still on the air talking to St. Louis, and, for a minute, I
wasn't sure what to do.

Then I remembered Bob Prince. I turned and shoved the
hot mike into his face, and he started talking. He was going
strong when I left to follow Harwell.

I ploughed down the aisle, trying to keep from falling over squirming, screaming fans, and just before I reached the field our statistician, Clay Felker, caught up with me.

"Clay," I gasped, "did you see it? Did you see it?"

"No, I didn't," he said. "I was too busy watching you. What a show you put on."

"I still don't believe it," I yelled. "I don't believe it . . ."

And, as we hurried across the field, passing cartwheeling kids and screeching men and women, I repeated it over and over—"I don't believe it—I don't believe it—"

We finally reached the clubhouse steps, and I must have taken them three at a time. When we got inside I could hear Prince's voice coming over the loudspeaker, but Ernie had everything ready for me. The engineer gave Prince the signal to cue me in, and his final spastic gurgle was a masterpiece of hometown loyalty.

"The Giants won the pennant," he said, "but remember—Ralph Kiner is still the home run champion of the National League—and now—Russ Hodges—"

Of course, nothing that went on in the clubhouse that afternoon made sense. The place was a bedlam. Durocher, his throat constricted and his voice hoarse from the stranglehold Stanky had held on him, dashed back and forth, patting guys on the back one minute and pointing at Bobby Thomson the next. Thomson, his face fixed in a happy grin that looked as if it would never come off, stood in front of his locker without making a move to take off his uniform.

"He did it—he did it—" Leo said in a squeaking voice that sounded as if it were just changing. Then he rushed Thomson, put his arms around him, and danced back along the line of ballplayers, hugging and croaking congratulations. Every once in a while, he came back and hugged Thomson again.

Horace Stoneham came in and embraced Durocher, and then the two went back to Thomson and there were more hugs, while Bobby, still in a roseate daze, barely moved. I stood on a trunk, trying to describe the scene, as Ernie rounded up the players for me, but nobody talked coherently. Paul Richards, the White Sox manager, who had come into town to cover the World Series for his hometown newspaper in Waxahachie, Texas, walked over to Leo, shook hands, and said, "You had it all the way." Bill Rigney yelled over and over, "It's in the clubhouse! It's in the clubhouse!"

Roy Campanella came in and shook hands all around, then quietly left. So did Walter O'Malley, the Dodgers' president. I thought of Ralph Branca. The last I had seen of him, he was sitting on the steps of the Dodgers' clubhouse, his head in his hands, and I wondered what the poor guy was doing now. Chuck Dressen walked in and congratulated Durocher. Ford Frick, the new baseball commissioner, and Warren Giles, the new National League president, came in, their faces wreathed in smiles.

Nobody thought about the World Series. That started the next day at Yankee Stadium, but, as far as the Giants were concerned, it was utterly anticlimactic. They weren't a bit upset when they lost it, four games to two, for they couldn't really believe they were in it to begin with. And all through the series, I couldn't either.

One day the following April, I was driving to Ebbets Field with Feeney and Buzzy Bavasi, the Dodgers' general manager, another Westchester neighbor of mine. After we crossed the Bronx-Whitestone Bridge, I got flagged down by a cop for speeding. I pulled up to the side of the road and said, "Don't worry, boys. As soon as this guy sees who I am, he'll let us go."

I handed over my license and waited for a smile of recognition. But the cop, after peering at it, just began writing a ticket.

"Hey, mister," I said, "what's that for?"

"I'm sorry I can't throw the book at you, you screaming maniac," he said. "I'm a Dodgers' fan and you made me run my motorcycle off the road when Bobby Thomson beat my bums with his lucky homer. Cost me fifteen bucks and I've been looking for you ever since."

Then he handed me the ticket, and I knew it had all happened. The Giants really had won the pennant on a storybook homer by Bobby Thomson.

The cop had made a believer of me at last.

Chapter 11

I hope some kind soul has remembered to put a gravestone on third base at Bears Stadium in Denver, bearing the legend: "Here lies the 1952 pennant hopes of the New York Giants," for it was there that Monte Irvin broke his right ankle two weeks before the season began.

Denver is one of America's loveliest cities, but its beauty has been lost on me ever since. Its fresh, clean air and breathtaking scenery are obscured by the unforgettable sight of Irvin writhing around at third base and Willie Mays on hands and knees, beating his fists into the ground and weeping like a child who has just seen his father hit by a truck.

It had been a good spring training up to then, with Willie the life of the party. He had never been west of Kansas City, and the mountains and cactus and perpetual sunshine of Arizona fascinated him. So did the very idea of being in training with a big league ball club, which was also a new experience for him.

Beyond everything else, the Phoenix people couldn't do enough for the Giants. They took a proprietary interest in everyone, and parties were being thrown for us all over the place. Every ballplayer was a celebrity, with Bobby Thomson the biggest of all. But everyone came in for his share of attention, and that was what interested Willie most.

"They *know* me, Russell," he said one day in his high-pitched voice.

"You're an important guy," I said.

"Not that important," he said.

He got a kick out of everything, even when he was the butt of a practical joke. Once I pulled one on him that broke him up, although it took him a few minutes before he was physically able to laugh.

The Chamber of Commerce had a real western party for us one night, featuring barbecued beef, pinto beans, corn pone, and tiny, viciously hot Mexican peppers. Most people have to eat those things with caution, but my mouth must be made of cast iron. The hotter they are, the better I like them.

Willie was sitting beside me, and when I popped a couple into my mouth, he said, "What are you eating, Russell?"

"These are sweet little peppers, Will," I said. "They're just wonderful—they melt right in your mouth."

"Well," said Mays, "I guess I'll have some then."

So he took three or four, put them into his mouth, and began chewing. The next thing I knew, he seemed to be going right up to the top of the mountain. He sputtered for fifteen minutes before he said, "Russell, I won't ever again believe anything you tell me."

He still laughs about it.

As spring training progressed, Durocher grew more and more confident. Eddie Stanky had become manager of the St. Louis Cardinals, but Davey Williams, with the help of Alvin Dark beside him, was doing an excellent job at second base. Leo had both Bobby Thomson and Hank Thompson working out at third base, planning to use one there and the other in the outfield. Mays and Irvin would be regular outfielders, with Mueller in and out. Westrum was the number one catcher, and the pitching staff still looked good.

But after Irvin broke his leg, Durocher had to start juggling the outfield around. Despite this, the Giants got off to a great start, winning sixteen of their first eighteen games, and taking an early lead in the pennant race. When we swept a three-game series from the Dodgers in late May, we were two and a half games in front of them.

The day after that series ended, Mays was drafted into the Army. Willie had never really hit his stride at the plate, for he was batting only .236 at the time he left, but he would have pulled out of that sooner or later, and his inspirational value was tremendous. The ball club went into a tailspin, lost six of the next eight games, fell behind the Dodgers, and never caught up.

Sal Maglie, who got away to a fabulous start, winning the first nine games he pitched, came up with a sore back in July. So did Larry Jansen. With those two below par, we didn't have a chance. We were lucky to finish second, four and a half games behind Brooklyn.

The 1953 season was worse. With poor pitching and no Willie, we finished fifth. As soon as Durocher realized we weren't going to win the pennant, he lost interest in the club.

One day in August I said, "Well, Leo, we've got a chance to finish second."

"What good is second?" he said. "If we can't win, I don't care where we finish."

When Leo didn't have a winner, he wouldn't even get mad at anybody. One day at Ebbets Field in early September, Jackie Robinson, with whom Durocher had been feuding ever since Leo left the Dodgers, strolled by him and, sniffing, said, "Hey, Leo, you still wearing Laraine's perfume?"

The crack, a reference to Durocher's use of exotic-smelling lotions, was an old Jackie Robinson gag, guaranteed to get a rise out of Leo. But this time it didn't. Durocher just said, "Don't bother me," and walked away.

One day he said to Dark, "Alvin, you run the ball club."

"What do you mean, Skip?" Dark said.

"Just what I say—you're the manager today," Durocher said.

So Dark ran the club, naming the pitcher and making all the decisions, while Durocher sat in the dugout and relaxed. He had Westrum run the club another day and Lockman another. Leo hardly watched the ball game.

Once I asked him, "Don't you really care what happens to the team?"

"Not this year," he said.

"Next year?" I said.

"Ah—next year, Russ," he said. "Next year is different."

"Next year" was 1954.

It began with a trade that seemed routine at the time. In early February the Giants swapped Bobby Thomson and Sam Calderone, a young catcher, to the Milwaukee Braves for Johnny Antonelli, Don Liddle, Ebba St. Claire, and Billy Klaus. The big man in the deal was Thomson. The Braves wanted a right-handed power-hitting outfielder, and he was it. The Giants needed left-handed pitching help, but how much they could expect from Antonelli and Liddle was problematic.

Antonelli had been a sixty-five thousand dollar bonus baby in 1948 who, after three nondescript seasons with the Braves while they were in Boston, had gone into the Army for two years. By the time he got out, the ball club had been transferred to Milwaukee. In 1953, Antonelli had been a starting pitcher there, but hardly a hotshot, ending up with twelve wins and twelve defeats. But Leo liked him and thought he could be a big winner. Liddle was a fair to middlin' southpaw relief pitcher, St. Claire a journeyman catcher, and Klaus a utility infielder.

Who could foresee that Antonelli would be a twenty-one-game winner and Liddle would do a great job both starting and in relief? For that matter, who could foresee that Thomson, like Irvin two years before, would break his leg in spring training and do the Braves practically no good at all?

The 1954 season also marked the return of Willie Mays after nearly two years in the Army. Spring training had just started when he got out. We had a Negro scout named Frank Forbes who was very close to Willie. He was assigned to meet Mays at Fort Eustis, Virginia, take him to Washington, and see that he got on an airplane for Phoenix.

It was a cold day and Mays had no overcoat. Forbes gave Willie his and kept himself warm by stuffing newspapers under his jacket. When he stepped off the plane in Washington, he looked as if he were hiding an arsenal, and the F.B.I. swooped down on him. Just a day or two before that some Puerto Ricans had fired shots on the floor of the House of Representatives, wounding several congressmen.

Forbes finally managed to explain the situation and everything ended happily. The scout stayed with Willie until the flight took off for Phoenix around midnight. There were no jets then and the plane was a milk run to the West Coast, so the trip took about thirteen hours. Garry Schumacher met Mays at the airport. All Willie had with him was a little overnight case.

"Give me your baggage checks," Garry said. "We'll get the stuff outside and take a cab to the ball park."

"I don't have any baggage checks," Willie said. "Everything but this is being shipped."

All he had in the overnight case was a toothbrush, a razor, a glove, and a pair of new baseball shoes.

When Mays arrived at the ball park, the team was working out on the field, and only Eddie Logan, the clubhouse man, was in sight in the locker room. He let out a whoop and that brought in Sal Maglie, dripping wet, from next door.

"Hey, Sal," Willie yelled, "where you been?"

"In the shower," Maglie said.

"Just what I thought," Willie said. "Knocked out again."

Irvin and Thompson walked in, followed by Freddy Fitzsimmons, the coach. By then Willie was in uniform, and he couldn't wait to get out to the field. The first man to spot him there was Lou Effrat of the New York *Times*, who yelled, "Hey, Leo, here comes your pennant."

Everybody rushed over then, but Leo got there first. After practically wrestling Willie to the ground, he yelled, "O.K., as long as you're going to win me a pennant, you might as well get started now."

There was an intrasquad game on, and Willie went right to center field. He hadn't been out there thirty seconds when the batter belted a tremendous blast that was ticketed for three bases. Willie turned, ran for it, and hauled it down. He hit a single his first time up and walloped a long home run his last. At that point, Leo just sat back and said, "Let's avoid the rush and get those World Series tickets printed right now."

Another interesting development in the 1954 season was the emergence from obscurity of James Lamar Rhodes, the colossus known as Dusty. He had been with us for two years, but hadn't made much of a dent on the rest of the baseball world. Dusty was a real character.

The first time I laid eyes on him was the day he reported to us in Cincinnati in 1952. The Giants got him from Nashville of the Southern Association, where he was hitting .347 and had belted eighteen home runs in ninety games. A left-handed pull hitter, he would come in very handy, especially at the Polo Grounds, where it was only 258 feet to the right-field foul pole.

He was a big, loud, lovable guy, who walked around saying, "I ain't never going to make a living with the leather, but just put a bat in my hand and I'll be fine."

He was right. If Dusty could have fielded, he might have been a great ballplayer, and if Grandmother had had wheels, she might have been a freight train. But how that man could hit a baseball!

One day, soon after he reported in 1952, Durocher sent him up as a pinch-hitter in St. Louis against Wilmer (Vinegar Bend) Mizell, who had a prodigious fast ball, and was just wild enough to keep hitters on their toes.

His first pitch came zipping in high and inside. As Rhodes jumped away from it, his cap flew in the air and the ball actually went between it and the top of his head. Most guys would be very wary after that, but not Rhodes. He belted the next pitch off the right-field screen for a double. When he came back to the bench later, he said calmly, "That fellow out there—he doesn't have very good control, does he?"

During that first year, Rhodes hit ten home runs in sixty-seven games and made nine errors in fifty-six games in the outfield. This was about par for his course, so there wasn't much Durocher could do but take the best possible advantage of Dusty's power. Rhodes did a little better in 1953, but broke no records for flawless fielding. One day in August he smashed three home runs in succession off three different Cardinal pitchers. He had thirty-eight hits that year, eleven of them homers.

If Rhodes could have fielded well enough to play regularly in 1954, he might have broken all records for runs batted in, because he piled up forty-eight in only 164 times at bat. But much as Durocher loved to see Rhodes hit, he couldn't break up his outfield of Irvin, Mays, and Mueller too often, since Irvin had hot streaks and the other two pasted the ball hard all year. Occasionally, when Irvin cooled off, Dusty went to left field, a move which Leo used to describe as a calculated risk.

Even though he practically had to do double duty when Rhodes was in the outfield, Mays got a big kick out of him. "Dusty," he said, "you just keep on hitting that ball and I'll just keep on fielding it. Don't worry about left field at all. If anybody hits one out there, you stand still and I'll catch it for you."

Dusty had some strange expressions, apparently colloquialisms from his native Alabama. Some weren't the least bit humorous, but they tickled Rhodes so much that everybody laughed just watching him hee-haw all over the place. Typical was his description of Roger Bowman, a young pitcher with a pronounced herky-jerky motion. "That Bowman!" Dusty roared, "he's the funniest thing since nickel hamburgers."

Dusty's favorite subject was a Navy buddy named Ack-Ack. They missed their ship in Shanghai one time, and didn't catch up with it for three months. "We kept going down to the dock looking for it," he told me, "but it was a long time coming back. By the time we finally made it, we'd each piled up so many extra hours of duty that we came home with housemaid's knee. I'll bet we were the only guys in the Navy who mopped our way across the Pacific."

One day as we sat together on an airplane back to New York, Dusty said, "Russ, I wonder where old Ack-Ack is now."

"Since I never knew Ack-Ack," I said, "I haven't the faintest idea."

"I sure hope he's not in some pen," Dusty said. "He was a pretty good old boy, so what I want to do is look me up a good lawyer because if Ack-Ack is in the pen, I want to get him out."

"What makes you think he's in the pen?" I said.

"Well, *maybe* he isn't," Dusty said, "but you don't know Ack-Ack."

We started the 1954 season with a lineup that rarely changed except to make room for Rhodes once in a while. Lockman was on first, Williams on second, Dark at short, Thompson on third, Irvin in left, Mays in center, and Mueller in right. Wes Westrum caught about two-thirds of the games, with Ebba St. Claire filling in during the early part of the season and Ray Katt later. Antonelli, Maglie, Liddle, and Ruben Gomez were our most reliable starters, and we got remarkable mileage out of Hoyt Wilhelm and Marv Grissom in the bullpen.

The season began in a mad scramble, with the Giants just off a pace set by four other clubs, the Dodgers, the Phillies, the Cardinals, and the Braves. By early June, with Mays murdering the ball and Antonelli mowing down almost everyone he faced, the Giants began rolling. When we swept a three-game series from Brooklyn at the end of the month, we completed a run of twenty-four victories in twenty-eight games, and that put us four games in front of the pack.

For a while Mays had the whole country talking about Babe Ruth's 1927 home run record of sixty. At the All-Star break, Willie had thirty-one and was ten games ahead of Ruth's pace, but he slackened off in the second half of the season when he hit only ten more.

When I asked him if the thought of Ruth's record bothered him during that period, he said it didn't. "I don't go up there trying for home runs," he said. "I just want base hits. I know if I get enough of them, some will be homers. But if I ever really tried for homers, it'd cost me in hits."

In mid-season, Antonelli ran up an eleven-game winning streak, two or three of them in clutches. We threatened to slip a couple of times after the All-Star Game, but Johnny was always the stopper who got us back on the right track. Finally, with his twenty-one wins and seven losses and his 2.29 earned-run average, he was the top pitcher of the National League.

We were never less than three and a half games in front during the last half of the season. Durocher was his usual nervous, hard-driving self, but he was a lot easier to get along with as a front-runner than as a chaser.

"They've got to catch us," he said. "Let them worry."

Appropriately enough, Sal Maglie clinched the pennant for us in Brooklyn on September 20. We coasted home five games in front of the Dodgers, making it look so easy that there was none of the suspense or excitement of 1951.

The only question left on the last day of the season was who would win the batting championship. Mays, Mueller, and Duke Snider of the Dodgers were so close together that they all had a shot at it. We played in Philadelphia that afternoon, while the Dodgers were at home entertaining the Pirates. We could see how Mays and Mueller were doing, and Clay Felker kept their averages up to date as they came to bat. In order to keep tabs on Snider, we opened a telephone line from our radio booth to Ebbets Field.

It was no contest. Willie wore out Robin Roberts, the Phillies' pitcher, who got him out only once during an eleven-inning game which we finally won. On his other five trips to the plate, Willie walked twice and hit a single, a double, and a triple. That boosted him to .345 and gave him the title. Mueller had a single and a double in six times up to finish second at .342. Snider, hitless three times, finished a point behind Mueller.

Durocher was almost as happy about Mays winning the batting crown in his first full season in the National League as he was about winning the pennant. Because Leo could pass up no chance to make Willie look good, he inadvertently damned Mueller with faint praise while introducing Don during a civic reception to the team just before the World Series. Durocher might have said any one of a number of nice things about Mueller—that he led both leagues in hits with 212, that he was a great clutch hitter, that he was the most consistent batter on the ball club, that he could always be depended upon, that he was the son of a former big-league ballplayer. Instead, Leo said, "Here's the man who just lost the batting championship to Willie Mays."

The Indians broke the Yankees' stranglehold on the American League pennant that year, and came to New York for the first two games of the World Series. For seven innings, the opener was a fine pitching duel between Maglie and Bob Lemon. Going into the Cleveland half of the eighth, with the score 2–2, Maglie began to sag. After he walked Larry Doby to start the inning and Al Rosen singled to deep short, sending Doby to second, Durocher yanked Maglie for Don Liddle, who faced the left-handed Vic Wertz. Wertz tied into the first pitch and belted one which would have been a homer almost anywhere except the Polo Grounds. It was headed for deep center field, and everybody started running at once.

The moment the ball was hit, Mays turned his back on home plate and dashed madly toward the bleachers. He glanced over his shoulder once or twice without slackening speed, then, as his cap fell off, reached far in front of him and made a fantastic catch. Doby had started for third base, but held up in time to return to second and tag up. Rosen, who had rounded second base, had to go all the way back to keep from getting doubled up. He retraced his tracks fast, for, without wasting a motion, Mays spun around and gunned the ball to first base. The throw, fast and accurate, came within a whisker of nailing Rosen, who barely made it in time.

The huge crowd was so stunned that, for a moment, nobody made a sound. Then, as Willie casually bent to pick up his cap, there was a thunderous roar, and the buzz that followed lasted until the inning was over.

That catch not only saved the ball game, but seemed to take all the fight out of the Indians. They failed to score in the inning, and the game remained tied at the end of the ninth. When the Giants came up in the last of the tenth, it was still all even. With one out, Mays walked and stole second, and when Lemon passed Thompson purposely, Durocher sent Rhodes up to bat for Irvin.

Dusty wasted no time. He swung on Lemon's first pitch, a curve, and blooped it toward right field. The ball traveled in a high, lazy arc, and found a home in the lower deck of the grandstand, barely inside the foul line. As a home run, it was hardly a whizzer, but as a run-producer it was as good as a six-hundred-foot blast. Dusty chased his two mates home and the Giants won the ball game, 5–2.

After the game, I asked Mays, "Do you think that was the greatest catch you ever made?"

He grinned and said, "Now, Russell, you know better than that. The one I made off Skinner was tougher. So was the one off Furillo. This one just *looked* tough, but I had it all the way."

I remembered the other two catches well, particularly the one off Bob Skinner, which Willie had made just a few weeks earlier. The big Pittsburgh rookie hit a vicious smash into the same place where Wertz's had gone, but on a much lower trajectory. Mays didn't have time to turn his back and run. He had to race at an angle and spear it going away. I don't know how he caught up with that ball, and neither does he.

I doubt if any outfielder alive, with the possible exception of Jimmy Piersall, could have made that play.

The one off Carl Furillo was made in 1952, just before Mays went into the Army. Billy Cox was on third base at the Polo Grounds when Furillo hit a line drive into right center. Mays had his back to the infield when he jumped up to catch the ball, and he positioned himself to throw while still in the air. The moment his feet hit the ground, he gunned the ball on a line to Wes Westrum at the plate. Cox, trying to score after the catch, was so surprised he didn't even slide, and was an easy out. Nobody—but nobody—could have made *that* one. When someone asked Manager Chuck Dressen of the Dodgers about it, Dressen said, "I'd have to see him do it again before I'll believe it."

But neither the Skinner catch nor the one off Furillo saved a World Series game or turned a World Series tide, and the one off Wertz did. Why should I—or Willie either—try to rub any of the glamor off what is accepted by many experts as the greatest World Series catch in history?

Dusty Rhodes broke up the second game also. He batted for Irvin with men on first and third, nobody out, and the Indians leading, 1–0, in the last of the fifth. Dusty hit a line shot to center off Early Wynn, scoring Mays with the tying run and sending Thompson to third. Thompson later scored when the Indians missed a double play. Rhodes remained in the ball game and hit a four-hundred-fifty-foot blast over the right-field stands in the seventh inning to give the Giants a 3–1 victory. Dusty's first homer might have been a little Chinese, but the second was as American as Indian pudding.

Rhodes continued his rampage in the third game, at Cleveland's Municipal Stadium. Batting for Irvin for the third time in the Series, he came up in the third inning with the bases full, one out, and the Giants ahead, 1–0, and whacked Mike Garcia's first pitch for a base hit that scored two runs. The Giants went on to win that one, 6–2.

In the locker room after the game, I said, "Dusty, how come you hit that first pitch all the time?"

"My old man always told me to be thrifty," he said. "He told me I shouldn't ever be wasteful, even of time. I was just doing what he told me."

He looked at me and grinned. "Say, Russ," he said, "can they hear the World Series in the pen?"

"Why, sure," I said.

"That's good," he said. "I just hope old Ack-Ack is listening —if he's in the pen, that is."

The fourth game turned out to be the last. We jumped into an early lead and won an easy 7–4 victory to wrap it all up. It was the first time in forty years and only the second time in history that a National League team had won the World Series in four straight games.

It was great for Leo Durocher and great for the Giants. The man and the team came home on the crest of a wave of popularity.

If anybody had suggested Leo would be through with the Giants in a year, I'd have said he was crazy.

And if anybody had suggested the Giants would be through with New York two years after that, I'd have said he was crazier.

But both things happened.

Chapter 12

The Dodgers won the first ten games they played in 1955, lost two out of the next three, then won eleven more in a row, and that was the end of the pennant race. While they were galloping home 13½ games in front of the Braves, life at the Polo Grounds kept going from bad to worse. We were lucky to finish third.

Everything went wrong. Henry Thompson, who had never been a fancy Dan around third base, couldn't find his way around there any more, and played there very little. Davey Williams, who had taken Stanky's place at second, developed an arthritic condition in his back and was in agony a good part of the time. Alvin Dark broke a rib in August, and the day after he returned to action suffered a shoulder separation that finished him for the year.

Monte Irvin was through. Waived out of the big leagues in June, he went to our Minneapolis farm club, where Bill Rigney was learning the intricacies of managing. Sal Maglie no longer seemed to have it, and was sold to Cleveland. Johnny Antonelli, not nearly the pitcher he had been in 1954, lost more games than he won. So did Ruben Gomez.

But Willie Mays didn't slip. Besides making his usual quota of tremendous plays in the outfield, he led the majors with fifty-one home runs, batted in 127 runs, and was second in league batting percentage to Richie Ashburn. Willie was the only man on the team who could be consistently depended upon. The others had good days and bad, but more of the latter.

Those of us who were close to Leo Durocher thought he did the best managing job of his career that year. One day, while discussing the Dodgers, somebody remarked that Walter Alston was doing a great job with them.

"That's true enough," Alvin Dark said, "but nobody's doing as great a job as Leo. As far as I'm concerned, he's the Manager of the Year."

I'll never know how Durocher kept us in third place. He used everything but masking tape in patching up the infield, and never stopped juggling pitchers around. This certainly wasn't his kind of team, but he stayed with it all the way. Ordinarily, he would have stopped worrying as soon as he realized he couldn't possibly win the pennant. But Leo knew this was his last year, and he didn't want to bow out a second-division manager. At the end of the season he resigned to go into television.

Our troubles weren't confined to the ball field. The team couldn't be blamed entirely for an attendance drop of over three hundred thousand. People were staying away from the Polo Grounds more than from the Giants. The place was outmoded, badly located, and short of parking facilities.

Horace Stoneham didn't complain, but he must have been watching with interest the moves being made over in Brooklyn by Walter O'Malley, the Dodgers' president. Even though he had a winner, O'Malley had problems similar to ours. His club needed a new ball park as badly as we did.

In August, O'Malley made a double-barreled announcement that shook up the whole town. The Dodgers would play seven of their 1956 home games in Jersey City's Roosevelt Stadium. And under no circumstances would they continue to use Ebbets Field after the 1957 season.

Being neither a prophet nor a mind reader, I had no idea at the time that this meant anything to us. I still don't know what Horace Stoneham was thinking. I do know that he wanted to start rebuilding the ball club around Mays as quickly as possible. His first move was to appoint Bill Rigney the Giants' manager. Rig had just won an American Association pennant at Minneapolis, and several of his players there might well be the Giants of the future.

But the non-playing manager who can hit and run and field for his ballplayers hasn't been invented yet, and the Giants got worse instead of better. Mays, hurt badly enough by the departure of Irvin, was lost without Durocher. His .296 batting average and thirty-six home runs in 1956 would have been great for an ordinary ballplayer, but were well below Willie's capabilities.

The infield problem didn't change, and Rigney had to keep fooling around with it, trying to make it jell. Antonelli regained much of his 1954 form and won twenty games, but he couldn't carry the whole pitching load himself.

Obviously, something had to be done in a hurry, so Stoneham went into the open market. In June, he cooked up a trade with Frank Lane, the Cardinals' general manager, which turned out to be the biggest of the year. Dark, Liddle, Katt, and Lockman went to St. Louis for Red Schoendienst, Jackie Brandt, Bill Sarni, and a couple of pitchers.

The Giants parted with Dark reluctantly, but room had to be made for Daryl Spencer, a fine young shortstop. Schoendienst would plug up the hole at second base. Sarni was a promising young catcher and Brandt an outfielder who appeared to have a good future.

But nothing helped, and we finished sixth. In the meantime, there were a lot of rumors circulating about the West Coast being ripe for big league baseball, but we didn't pay much attention to them. The West Coast had been ripe for several years, and nobody had done much about it. The rumors weren't new—there were just more of them.

Then O'Malley suddenly dropped another bombshell. He sold Ebbets Field to a real estate operator and repeated that the Dodgers would leave there at the end of the 1957 season. Up to then, many people thought he had been bluffing. Now everyone knew he meant business and, for the first time, there were stories all over town linking the Dodgers and Los Angeles. When asked about them, O'Malley said the team would stay in Brooklyn if a suitable site for a new stadium could be found there.

We still didn't pay much attention. All the gossip was about the Dodgers. Nobody mentioned the Giants.

Not many people came out to see us play either. With the Yankees and the Dodgers headed for a repeat performance of their 1955 World Series, we were third horse in a three-horse town. The Polo Grounds was too peaceful for comfort. Since nobody else got excited about the Giants, we had a tough time getting excited about them ourselves.

My broadcasting partner was Bob Delaney, and we were later joined by Jim Woods. Sometimes all we heard was the sound of our own voices. There were times when the place was so quiet we had to speak softly to keep from interfering with each other, because the radio and television booths were side by side. Without the crowd noises in the background, our voices echoed back and forth like yodelers if we talked too loud.

We were sixth in the standings and last in the stands. Our attendance, the poorest in the National League, dipped below six hundred thirty thousand. I knew something would have to be done, but I had no idea that Stoneham had anything in mind beyond trying to make some deals that would help the ball club.

In February of 1957, the Dodgers bought Wrigley Field in Los Angeles. A month later, O'Malley invited the Los Angeles baseball writers to visit the Dodgers' spring training quarters in Vero Beach, Florida. He still maintained that the club would stay in Brooklyn if it could find a place to play, but his intentions were pretty obvious.

And still there were no rumors about the Giants.

Our season began on a frightening note when Bill Sarni, a twenty-nine-year-old athlete who had never been seriously sick before, had a heart attack on the first day of spring training. He had just come out to the field where reporters, photographers, and characters like me were milling around, all contributing to the confusion of opening day in Arizona.

I had just finished interviewing Tom Sheehan on my tape recorder when Sarni walked by. I stopped him and said, "How about talking into this with me for a few minutes?"

"Be glad to, Russ," he said.

He stood beside me, while I held the microphone between us. But before I could say a word, he suddenly moaned, clutched at his chest, dropped to the ground, and started writhing around as if he'd been shot. Doc Bowman got a stretcher out, and Sarni was rushed to the hospital. His ailment was first diagnosed as a mild heart condition, but then it was established that he had had a full-fledged heart attack which, of course, finished his baseball career before it was fairly started.

It also left us without anything resembling a first-string catcher. Sarni had done so well in the last part of 1956 that Rig had been depending on him for heavy duty behind the plate. Now Bill had a new problem to add to all the old ones. It promised to be—and was—a long, hard season.

The activity off the field was much more interesting. I first learned what to expect from Horace Stoneham, who called me into his office one day in May.

"Russ," he said, "do you want to move to California?"

"Give me an hour to pack," I said. "Are you serious?"

"Certainly," he said. "It looks as if we're going to San Francisco. There are a lot of loose ends, like getting everything in writing, but I don't anticipate any great problems."

"San Fran–cis–co," I rolled each syllable around on my tongue like a piece of candy. "You picked my favorite town."

He told me that Mayor George Christopher had come to New York personally to invite the Giants, and that the city was prepared to build a new ball park. He said that if the Dodgers went to Los Angeles, it would enable the two teams to continue the natural rivalry which had started in New York, but that he intended to go to California even if they didn't. And he warned me to keep my mouth shut.

"The deal isn't closed yet," he said. "Too much talk can be very harmful, so don't say a word. I told you about it so that it won't come as a complete surprise. Besides, you've got a house to sell, and this will give you time to put it on the market."

San Francisco! There was beauty and romance in its very name. I had been there many times for fights or football games and, like so many thousands of others, had long since fallen in love with the place. I envied the people who lived in the city, looked forward to every trip I made there, and was always sorry to leave. I hadn't been kidding when I told Horace it was my favorite town.

And my second favorite was New York. I had spent twelve wonderful years there. The idea of leaving shook me up a little, although it didn't really rock me. I had close ties in New York, but no roots. It wasn't my hometown, and this wouldn't be my first move from one city to another.

The shift would mean much more to men like Eddie Brannick and Garry Schumacher, to say nothing of Horace Stoneham himself. They had been born and brought up in New York and had never called any other place home. It must have given Stoneham a terrific wrench to make his decision.

Not until after I left his office did I realize that the National League would probably be left without a team in New York. That bothered me some because it meant I wouldn't be coming back very often. New York was the center of the radio and television advertising industry, the place where the big network shows were dreamed up, and a very convenient spot for a guy in my business to live.

All of this still wasn't enough to dampen my eagerness to go to San Francisco. Weighing the advantages of one town against the other, I still felt I was getting the best of the bargain.

Now that I knew what was going to happen, I began watching for developments. An important step was taken in late May when the league voted unanimously to permit the Giants and the Dodgers to move their franchises if they so desired. I expected that would set off a flood of new rumors involving us, but it didn't. While New York fans were beginning to take for granted that the Dodgers were going, they either didn't notice, didn't care, or didn't believe that they might lose the Giants too. The Polo Grounds crowds were as skimpy as ever. It didn't look as if many people would miss us.

Then, in mid-July, testifying before a congressional subcommittee investigating professional sports, Stoneham dropped his bombshell. The Giants, he said, were definitely leaving New York at the end of the 1957 season.

"My thinking," he told the subcommittee, "is that New York can't support three major league clubs. The baseball population is moving to the suburbs. The Board of Directors has discussed a move for the past four or five years. Our current location is such that it is impossible for us to operate profitably."

Later, in answer to a question, Horace said that the team's destination was not yet definite, but that "San Francisco has the inside track." At a press conference in New York the next day, he was even more specific. "I am going to recommend to my Board of Directors that we leave the Polo Grounds after this season," he said. "We have no chance to survive here."

Now the sleeping Giants' fans suddenly woke up. They met in streets, in subways, in buses, in taxis, in theaters, in restaurants, in bars, in night clubs, in stores, in barber shops, in shoeshine parlors, in sewers, in basements, in offices, in ambulances, in trucks, in hospitals, in police stations, in barges, in airplanes, in libraries, in hotels, in Fifth Avenue mansions, in Bowery flophouses, in the Bronx, in Manhattan, in Times Square, in Greenwich Village, in Stamford, in Westchester, in Jersey, and in every other nook and corner of, under, over, and near the city, weeping, wringing their hands, and gnashing their teeth at the injustice of it all.

They made speeches and wrote letters to the editor and phoned their friends and wired their congressmen, demanding in the names of Jim Mutrie and Mike Donlin and John McGraw and Christy Mathewson and Larry Doyle and Rube Marquard and Irish Meusel and Casey Stengel and Frankie Frisch and Bill Terry and Carl Hubbell and Mel Ott and Leo Durocher and Bobby Thomson and Peter Stuyvesant that the Giants stay in New York.

And they avoided the Polo Grounds like the plague.

When we returned from a western trip, the fuss was still going on. One night, when about five thousand fans were scattered around the premises in places where they were likely to make the least noise, somebody remarked, "The people of New York don't want a ball club. They want a monument."

That was one of the times Delaney, Woods, and I had to whisper. We might as well have been in Grant's tomb.

The final decision to move to San Francisco came in August. On the ninth, Stoneham received a long letter from Mayor Christopher, spelling out in detail exactly what the city would do for the Giants if they moved there. Most important was an agreement to build a new stadium accommodating between forty and fifty thousand people, with parking for about twelve thousand cars. While the new ball park was being built, the Giants would play in Seals Stadium.

Ten days later, eight of the nine Giants' directors approved the transfer, and Stoneham announced it at a press conference. He explained that the club was still operating in the black, but with attendance dropping, couldn't continue to do so. He couldn't see a resurgence of fan interest if we stayed at the Polo Grounds, so he thought it best to leave while there was still time.

The wailing and the weeping and the letters to the editor started dying down after that, and the crowds at the ball park were poorer than ever. Three days after the directors' meeting, 2600 showed up for a game with the Cubs, and 2300 came out a few days after that to watch us play the Reds. The pennant-bound Braves didn't exactly pack them in either —we had a total of twenty-five thousand for a two-game series.

The fight was over. Even the diehards were giving up.

On the next to last day of the season, 2768 people went through the Polo Grounds turnstiles to watch the Giants play the Pirates. But on the final day, nearly twelve thousand came out to say goodbye to the ancient institution that was the New York Giants, while the ghosts of John McGraw and all the others hovered over Coogan's Bluff.

We had a little ceremony at home plate before the game, where some of the old-timers tearfully stood to be introduced to the fans who had cared enough to make a last pilgrimage to the Polo Grounds. Larry Doyle was there, and Hooks Wiltse, and Moose McCormick, and Hans Lobert. Billy Jurges and Carl Hubbell were there, and Sal Maglie. Bobby Thomson and Whitey Lockman, back with the Giants, stood by, their caps in their hands, their faces somber, as though in the presence of death. Eddie Brannick, who had been with the Giants since he was thirteen and was prepared to go to San Francisco with them, stood with brimming eyes beside Mrs. John McGraw, who wept softly into a massive corsage.

Maybe some of the fans in the stands wept too—I don't know. I felt kind of funny myself.

But most of the Giants' ballplayers didn't. They watched curiously, their faces disinterested, their eyes blank. Their loyalties were with the Giants, not New York. Few of them lived anywhere near the city anyhow. It didn't matter to them where the ball club went.

The game itself was a dreadful spectacle. The Giants were anchored in sixth place, and the Pirates were seventh. Except for the second-base combination of Danny O'Connell and Daryl Spencer, our starting lineup was much the same as it had been in 1954—Lockman at first, Thomson at third, Mueller, Mays, and Rhodes in the outfield, Westrum catching, and Antonelli pitching. But it really wasn't the same team. All but Mays and Antonelli were near the end of the line.

Bob Friend threw a six-hitter at our rag, tag, and bobtail ball club, and the Pirates won, 9–1. Mays had two of the six hits. The rest were scattered.

At least we didn't have to whisper up in our booths. The crowd was noisier than usual, and it applauded every move the Giants made. The loudest yell was for Willie when he came up for the last time. When he grounded out, he heard more cheers than he had heard for many of his home runs that year.

After the game ended, a strange thing happened. Ignoring the usual warning to stay off the field until the ballplayers had gone to their clubhouses, the crowd surged from the stands and fanned out for souvenirs of every conceivable description. They uprooted home plate and hacked it up into little pieces. They unhitched the bases and fought over them. They hauled down the canopies over the two bullpens and pulled out the telephones. They ripped the green foam rubber covering off the fences and tore it apart. Some even scooped dirt up into paper bags or bottles to take home as mementos of the ball park that had been the home of the Giants for forty-six years.

All over the field, they yelled, "Stay, team, stay," and hundreds gathered at the foot of the clubhouse steps yelling, "We want Willie!"

I stood inside the locker room and waxed sentimental, speaking erroneously (who ever heard of the Mets then?) of the last ball game ever at the Polo Grounds—the last home run, the last strikeout, the last base on balls, the last appearance of the Giants or any other big league ball club there. I spoke of the clubhouse celebrations of happier days, and of the pictures on its walls, and of the memories that flooded back as we all wandered around there.

And I interviewed people, for this was a historic moment which meant a great deal to a great many old friends of the Giants. I felt pretty sad myself, for I'm just a fat little baby when I see something that once was great come to an end. It's not easy to preside over the death of a tradition.

But Bill Rigney couldn't have been happier. His home, in Walnut Creek, was just across the bay from San Francisco. He sat at his desk off the locker room, trying to sound doleful, but his heart was singing. Somehow, as we talked, he managed to look both forward and back with real sincerity.

"Sure it's a sad day, Russ," he said. "There are a lot of memories here—a lot of heartaches—and a lot of things we'll never want to forget." He stopped, and we could hear the crowd outside yelling, "Stay, team, stay" and "We want Willie!" He half-smiled and said, "We're tickled to death the way fans are with us—now. We're looking forward to a new team in a new city, but we won't forget the Polo Grounds." He stopped again and listened for a moment to the crowd outside. "We're looking forward to giving San Francisco the best team we can," he said.

"Maybe," I said, "the New York Giants' fans will be proud of the San Francisco Giants."

It was the first time I had ever said "San Francisco Giants" into a microphone, and my spine tingled.

I stopped beside old Hans Lobert, once one of the brightest of McGraw's great stars. He shook his head, and said slowly, "It's a sad day for me. The fans don't want to see the Giants leave. I hated to see them lose this last game." He halted, then added wistfully, "I wish they had won it."

I saw Buddy Kerr and Sid Gordon, both New Yorkers, both Giants' fans, both former Giants. They were deeply affected, but Kerr was philosophical. "It's kind of hard to come back to the Giants' clubhouse and see them leave forever," he said. "But I'm sure something had to be done." Gordon simply said, "I'm sorry—terribly sorry—to see them go."

Eddie Brannick, fighting back tears, was standing near the

door. The sixty-five-year-old team secretary had been with the Giants more than fifty-two years. Born and brought up in Hell's Kitchen, he had gone to work as an errand boy for John T. Brush, then the Giants' owner, in 1905. Brush was an invalid, and Eddie carried messages back and forth between him and John McGraw. Brannick was the epitome and symbol not only of the Giants, but of New York as well. He was a New Yorker from top to toe. I knew he would never be anything else, but he was going to San Francisco, for he couldn't bear the thought of not being where the Giants were.

"I don't have to ask you how you feel, Eddie," I said.

"No, Russ," he said, "no—you don't. But I love Horace and I loved his father before him. Anything anyone named Stoneham wants to do is all right with me."

We talked for a few moments about San Francisco, but Eddie had to fight to keep himself under control. I finally got a little smile out of him when I said, "You'll find a lot of wonderful Irishmen in San Francisco," but the smile didn't last. I guess he must have been thinking of all the wonderful Irishmen he was leaving in New York. He never really left. To this day, he still has his old apartment there.

The noise outside was beginning to subside, although I could still hear a few scattered shouts of "Stay, team, stay." We poked the television cameras out the clubhouse window, and took sweeping panoramic views of the ball park, while I got poetic.

"That, ladies and gentlemen—that is the Polo Grounds," I said, "historic in baseball memory—where the New York Giants played for forty-six years. So many friends—so many fans—so many players—Mathewson—Terry—Ott—Mays—so many others—"

I paused a moment, seeking a suitable windup, and found it in *Recessional*, by Rudyard Kipling.

"Yes, ladies and gentlemen—that is the Polo Grounds," I said. "The tumult and the shouting dies. The captain and the kings depart. Lest we forget—lest we forget—"

The New York Giants were dead.

The least I could do was try and give them a decent burial.

Chapter 13

Since I don't need anybody to tell me that the day will come when daisies will be planted on my chest, I'm glad I didn't work in Seals Stadium before the Giants got there because I would have had a disconcerting daily reminder. On the January afternoon in 1958 when I first saw the beautiful little watch-charm ball park, all green and cozy and freshly painted, workmen were dismantling a huge purple sign which had been over the clock in center field. It said: "Daphne Funerals—Eventually." The sign that replaced it, "Longine Watches," was more familiar and less intimidating.

After stopping in to say hello to Horace Stoneham, I went out to look at the radio booth. It was halfway up the single-tiered grandstand, and close enough to the seats so that we could carry on a conversation with anyone who happened to be around. But apparently the guys who were there before me weren't very good at ducking foul balls, because the booth was protected by shatterproof glass, which also gave it an aura of privacy.

The first thing I did was get those windows taken out. I'm fairly agile at dodging baseballs. Besides, I wanted to hear what was going on. I'd had enough peace and quiet at the Polo Grounds. It would be nice to be exposed to noise again.

As it turned out, we got pretty friendly with a couple who had season tickets right in front of us. The man's name was Jack, and he had an ulcer. Every day his wife brought brownies and milk in case he suffered an attack. We had a refrigerator in the booth, where we kept the milk. When

Jack was in distress, whoever wasn't on the air filled up a cup and gave it to him while he nibbled on a brownie and rooted for the Giants. It was real *gemütlich*.

My old radio partners stayed in New York, but I had no trouble finding a new one. Lon Simmons was the sports director of station KSFO, and he was just as much at home behind a microphone as I. The minute I met this six-foot-four-inch descendant of squaws and braves, I knew he was for me. Easygoing, almost constantly grinning, and the proprietor of a truly magnificent voice, he was a real pro, and we hit it off from the start. I don't remember ever having a serious argument with him, although we've had a million silly ones.

Lon and I hadn't met more than three or four times when I left for Phoenix. He was tied up with college basketball, and would join me in time to help broadcast weekend games back to San Francisco.

It started out as the toughest, bitterest, most confused spring training trip I ever knew, although everything leveled off nicely before it was over. To begin with we found we had a newspaper feud on our hands. The New York writers, who came to cover spring training as usual, wouldn't let go of the umbilical cord, and the San Francisco writers naturally resented it. The rivalry that resulted was bitter and embarrassing. We didn't want to slight our old friends of the metropolitan press, but we were the San Francisco Giants now, and our obligations were to the reporters from there. This caused some ill feeling, but there wasn't much we could do except try to be nice to everyone and hope for the best.

I gave Lon Simmons quite a turn the first time he saw me in Arizona. A few days before our broadcasts were to begin, I went to the hospital with a kidney stone. I could have gone right home after I got rid of it, but the doctor wanted me to stay overnight. Lon arrived with Franklin Mieuli the next day, and phoned from the airport. We had to be in Tucson that night for the opening game the next afternoon against the Cleveland Indians.

"What are you doing in the hospital?" Lon said.

"Waiting for you," I said. "Come on over and pick me up."

"Are you sure you're all right?" he said.

"Believe me," I said, "after what I've been through, I never felt better in my life."

"O.K.," he said. "We'll be right over."

As in most hospitals, this one had a rule that all discharged patients must be delivered to the front door in a wheelchair. When it was time for me to leave, they trundled me out, and an attendant stood by while I waited for Lon and Franklin. They pulled up in front of the place and Lon, white as death, rushed over to me and said, "Good Lord, you look terrible. I thought you said you were all right."

"I *am* all right," I said. "And I don't look any more terrible than usual. This is the way I always look."

"You've lost weight," he said.

"Maybe a little," I said. "I'll gain it back."

"Are you *sure* you can work?" he said.

"Positive," I said.

If he asked me that once, he asked me ten times on the way to Tucson. Neither of us was quite up to par as we pulled into town. I was one thin fat man and he was one scared Indian.

We had to do pre-game and post-game shows right from the ball park, so we tossed a coin and Lon drew the pre-game assignment. He had never broadcast a major league ball game, and his would be the first voice San Francisco fans would hear. Big as he was, he looked pretty forlorn out there on the field, waiting for Franklin Mieuli's signal that he was on the air. Bill Rigney was standing nearby talking to Eddie Stanky, then a Cleveland coach. Lon was going to interview both. He had never met either until I introduced him half an hour before.

Besides a full house of fans, he was being inspected by representatives of all four of our sponsors, Folger's Coffee, Falstaff Beer, White Owl Cigars, and Shell Oil. One bad bloop would send him right back to the studio in San Francisco, and he knew it.

But he carried it off well, and did a fine broadcast. Later he told me, "Before I ever got to say, 'Good afternoon, everyone,' I swallowed something that felt like a king-sized olive."

He was, as a matter of fact, better off than I, for he never had to catch himself calling the ball club anything but the San Francisco Giants. It's not easy to break the habits of a lifetime, and they had been the New York Giants to me as long as I could remember. Sure enough, when I got on the air the very first day in Arizona, I had to correct myself about three times.

Within the next few days, I must have received a hundred "Dear sir, you bum" letters from irate San Francisco fans who invited me in several different languages, including Cantonese, to go back to New York where I belonged.

I had the situation fairly well under control by the time we got back to San Francisco, but it was still far from licked. On opening day, I sat in that cozy little booth beside Lon, with "San Francisco Giants" and "Los Angeles Dodgers" scribbled all over the place so I surely wouldn't slip. Then I said: "Good afternoon, everyone, this is Russ Hodges with Lon Simmons about to bring you the first major league game ever played on the Pacific Coast—the opening game of the season between the San Francisco Giants and the Los Angeles Dodgers at the Polo Grounds—I mean Seals Stadium."

The game itself was an artistic success from every standpoint. A throng of 23,448 had the ball park creaking at the seams, and it was a roaring, happy, knowledgeable crowd, which saw everything it came to see. Ruben Gomez pitched a brilliant six-hit shutout as the Giants won a convincing 8–0 victory. The three rookies who played that day handled themselves like veterans. Orlando Cepeda, a right-handed batter, hit a booming home run to right, which was for him the opposite field. Jimmy Davenport got two hits and Willie Kirkland one, and both fielded their positions flawlessly.

That night, Lefty O'Doul, a San Francisco baseball immortal who once was the National League batting champion, heard the newsdealer at the corner of Powell and Geary yell, "New York Giants win opener."

"What's the difference?" Lefty said. "We're all walking around unconscious tonight."

I never heard of a newsdealer getting whomped for that kind of a boner, but when I pulled one I heard about it from fans and writers alike. San Francisco is a proudly provincial town and, although I have long since become as proudly provincial as anyone in it, there are some people there who haven't forgiven me yet. As recently as 1962, a *Chronicle* columnist, himself a transplanted New Yorker, raised the roof because on a trip east I referred to my home in San Francisco as "out there." He considered that a reflection of, in his own terms, "the view of the management," which, he went on, "leads to the inference that the Giants have never left New York, in their heart."

This, of course, was ridiculous. The Giants and the San Francisco fans have had a love affair going from the start, and it was equally intense on both sides. However, San Franciscans did resent references to or reminders of New York, which was why they welcomed Orlando Cepeda with open arms in 1958, somewhat at the expense of Willie Mays. They considered Cepeda their own hero and Mays New York's. Eventually they accepted Willie, too, but it took several years for him to shake off the curse of having been a star on the 1951 and 1954 Giants teams.

Willie and Whitey Lockman were the only holdovers from 1951 still with the team when it arrived in San Francisco from spring training in 1958, but Lockman had already lost his job to Cepeda. Orlando, a big, handsome slugging first baseman from Puerto Rico, had hit twenty-five home runs and batted .309 at Minneapolis the year before. In spring training, he was absolutely tremendous. Day after day, he stood at the plate and pulled booming drives to deep left and left-center field. He was the hottest thing in camp, of course, and had everybody talking about him.

A shy kid who spoke English with a heavy accent, Orlando was more or less adopted by Doc Bowman, the trainer.

"Orlando," Doc said one day, "you should talk better English."

"You teach me," Cepeda said.

"O.K.," Doc said. "We're in Fee–nicks."

"Fee–nicks," Orlando said. Then he walked around repeating, "Fee–nicks—Fee–nicks—Fee–nicks—"

He was thrilled when the Giants took him off the Minneapolis roster and put him on their own. So was everybody else. A slugging youngster like Orlando was exactly what we needed to get off to a good start in our new city.

We broke camp and started barnstorming home. Each day Orlando would walk up to Bowman and say, "Where we today, Doc?" Then he'd go out and belt a couple into the next county.

One day, in answer to the regular question, Doc said, "We're in Dee–Moyne, Orlando."

"Dee–Moyne–Dee–Moyne," Orlando said a couple of times, with his big grin. Then, "Where we go tomorrow, Doc?"

"O–ma–ha, Orlando."

"O–ma–ha. And, Doc, where we go then?"

"Then, Orlando," Doc said, "we go—whoosh—all the way to San Fran–cis–co."

Orlando grinned from ear to ear. "San Fran–cis–co—San Fran–cis–co—San Fran–cis–co—"

He liked the sound of it, and repeated it over and over. The next day I sat with him in the airplane.

"Russ," he said, "what's it like in San Fran–cis–co?"

"San Francisco is a beautiful city, Orlando," I said. "You'll like it there."

"You think so?" he said. Then he grinned and began repeating, "San Fran–cis–co. Bee–oo–ti–ful—" He said it over and over. He repeated it to everyone he met when he arrived there, was still repeating it after he hit a home run on opening day, and hadn't stopped repeating it at the end of the season, after he hit twenty-five home runs and piled up a .312 batting average. No wonder he knocked 'em dead there.

Cepeda was by far our most spectacular rookie, but he was only one of the finest crop of kids I've ever seen in one year. We had four who ranked as regulars, and a fifth who came along before the season was over.

Next to Cepeda, the one who made the biggest impression was Jimmy Davenport, who had the hands of a wizard and an arm like a whiplash. He locked up third base before we broke camp, and ended up by shoving Bobby Thomson clear off the ball club. Thomson was traded to the Cubs before we arrived home, and that time the hero of the 1951 miracle season was gone for good.

Willie Kirkland and Bob Schmidt were the other two kids

who made the ball club in Arizona. Kirkland was fresh out of the service, and he filled a gap in the outfield, where Mays was our only reliable starter. Schmidt was a rugged catcher who had been to Phoenix before but needed experience. He got it in 1957 at Minneapolis, and was ready by 1958.

Leon Wagner, another long-hitting outfielder, started the season on our Phoenix farm club, but later came to San Francisco, where he batted .318 and hit thirteen home runs in seventy-four games.

Rigney, with everything to gain and nothing to lose, wasn't afraid to pack the lineup with youngsters. As a result, the club was transformed overnight from a team of the past to a team of the future. The new faces also pleased the fans, for these boys had never played in New York. They belonged to San Francisco and nobody else.

I've always thought that the one thing that really sold us to the people of San Francisco was a fantastic ninth inning in a ball game against the Pirates in early May. It just missed its objective, but it still gave everyone, including yours truly, one of the thrills of the year.

Seals Stadium was jammed that day, but nobody was very happy because Pittsburgh piled up what appeared to be an absolutely prohibitive lead for Vernon Law, who had a four-hitter going into our half of the ninth inning. The score was then 11–1, and it didn't look as if we had the foggiest chance of catching up. But most of the people stuck around, and nearly saw a typical Giants' miracle.

Ray Jablonski, the leadoff man, singled, and so did Cepeda, who followed him. When Hank Sauer reached first on an error, the bases were full with nobody out. Then Kirkland popped up. So far, there was nothing to get excited about. Valmy Thomas, the catcher, Pete Burnside, the pitcher, and Eddie Bressoud were scheduled to come up next, but Rig

called on pinch-hitters for all three, and the results were
unbelievable.

The first one, Jim King, doubled, scoring Jablonski and
Cepeda. The second, Johnny Antonelli, also doubled, knocking in two more runs. And the third, Bob Speake, did the
same thing, scoring Antonelli. Three straight doubles by
three straight pinch-hitters, and the Pirates' lead was shaved
to 11–6.

Now there was a man on second with one out and, while
the crowd went wild, Manager Danny Murtaugh of the
Pirates yanked Law in favor of Curt Raydon, who walked
Willie Mays. When Daryl Spencer forced him at second,
sending Speake to third, the Pirates breathed a bit easier, but
the crowd didn't stop roaring.

Up came Jablonski for the second time, and he boomed
one out of the park, a three-run homer, making the score
11–9, with Cepeda the hitter. By this time the joint was really
jumping and, while I screamed into the microphone in a vain
attempt to be heard over the roars of the crowd, Murtaugh
rushed Ronnie Blackburn in to pitch for Pittsburgh.

When Cepeda unloaded another homer for the Giants'
ninth run of the inning, I thought everyone would go mad.
A crowd of twenty-three thousand makes an awful lot more
noise in a small ball park than in a big one, and even that's
exaggerated when you're right in the middle instead of in an
upstairs radio booth. We felt as if we were on the inside of a
snare drum, with the pounding and the howling coming at
us from all directions.

Now the score was 11–10, with Sauer up for the second
time. He walked. So did Bob Schmidt, who batted for Kirkland. When Jim Finigan, batting for King, hit a routine
ground ball to short, there was a long, low sigh, followed

by a sudden roar when Dick Groat bobbled the ball. He couldn't get rid of it, and the bases were loaded.

Antonelli was due up for the second time, but Rig yanked him too, sending Don Taussig up in his place. Taussig took two strikes, then sent an Alphonse-Gaston fly ball up behind second base—one of those pop-ups which anyone can catch but nobody wants. At the last minute, Bill Mazeroski, the second baseman, lunged and barely managed to hang on to the ball. That saved the 11–10 victory for the Pirates, but the fans didn't go home mad that day.

By then they cared little about the result. The only thing that counted was that they had seen the Giants get up off the floor and come within a whisker of winning an impossible ball game. It was prime proof that the Giants of San Francisco were just as unpredictable as the Giants of New York had been. No matter how hopeless the cause, they couldn't be counted out until the ball game was all over.

From then on, we could do no wrong. And, as a matter of fact, we didn't. Instead of floundering around as we had the year before, we were in the thick of the pennant race until after the All-Star Game. We finally finished third, which was far better than anyone expected.

The ball club was accepted, but I still had to watch my p's and q's. I didn't realize until I'd been around town awhile just how popular my partner Lon Simmons was, especially in his hometown of Fresno, which was on our network. Our official designation might have been "Russ Hodges and Lon Simmons," but in Fresno it was "Lon Simmons and Russ Hodges."

One day we were playing the Dodgers in the last game of a series in the Los Angeles Coliseum. We were due to fly home the following morning, but Lon had a business deal cooking that he could close if he got into town by nine.

When he told me about it, I said, "Go on up there tonight. You do the first part of the game and I'll finish up."

We agreed not to say anything about it, because someone might have objected. Lon left after doing the seventh inning, and I picked the game up from there. It was all tied up, but I figured it would be a routine ball game.

It was still tied at the end of the ninth, and we went into extra innings. Stan Williams was pitching for the Dodgers, and as we went into the tenth, I said, in the course of my remarks, "Williams looks pretty good, doesn't he, Lon?" then continued with my broadcast.

Williams got out of the inning, and the Dodgers came up for their half of the tenth. "Say, Lon," I said, "here comes Wally Moon. Real tough hitter"—and I went right on talking.

The tenth inning ended and we went into the eleventh. During a lull, I said, "Lon, can you make out who that is in the bullpen?" After the Dodgers' pitcher retired the side, I said, "Great inning for Williams again, wasn't it, Lon?"

The game went on and on, and the longer it lasted the more I referred to Lon. Nothing happened in the twelfth, or the thirteenth. As we came up for our half of the fourteenth, I said, "Lon, it's been a great ball game. Do you think we can settle it now?"

Finally, in the fourteenth, Davenport came up and belted a home run. "Bye bye baby," I yelled. "Hey, Lon, how did you like that?"

When Mays followed with another homer, I came up with another "Bye bye baby," then turned to the empty chair beside me and said, "Back to back, Lon! Wasn't that something?"

That was the ball game, and we went home the next morning.

And all week long, I was flooded with indignant mail from Fresno, accusing me of keeping their boy off the air during an exciting ball game. The unkindest cut of all came from Lon himself.

"Fat man," he said, when we met at the ball park the next night, "how come you're such a mike hog?"

Chapter 14

Sponsors are my bread and butter, the cream in my coffee, the frosting on my cake, the warp and woof of my existence. I love them dearly and I can't live without them, for an announcer without a sponsor is like an airplane without wings. I do everything I can to keep them happy. Bad as I am on commercials, I give them all of what little I have. I mention them whenever the occasion arises, and sometimes even when it doesn't.

One football season when I was working for Pabst, they had a slogan that went "Thirty-three fine brews blended into one swell beer," so we had about every other play taking place on the thirty-three-yard line. There used to be thirty-three-yard gains, thirty-three-yard passes, thirty-three-yard kicks, and we even had substitutes running out thirty-three yards to get to the field from the bench. And, of course, each time we were reminded of those thirty-three fine brews.

One of our present sponsors, Dual Filter Tareytons, a product of the American Tobacco Company, features the "white ring around the tip," so every once in a while we mention the next batter. He's crouching in the on-deck circle which is a white ring, and of course that always reminds us of the "white ring around the tip" of every Dual Filter Tareyton.

One night years ago, before television, I did a fight so horrible that the customers were singing "Waltz Me Around Again, Willie" and I nearly came out with "Danny Boy" myself. For four rounds, all I could say were things like,

"Butch swings and misses and they clinch," or "Biff ducks and they clinch," or "the referee moves in to separate them." Then I got a note from the advertising agency that said, "If you can't make this sound better, we're through."

The next round was no better than the others, but I barked into the microphone, "Butch lands a left to the body—a right to the jaw—oh—here comes Biff with a terrific belt to the chin and Butch is in trouble—no—he comes back with a right—and a right—and a *third* right—and Biff's nose is bleeding—"

Just before the round ended, a guy poked me from behind and said, "Hey, mister, where's that fight you're talking about? I'd like to see it too."

At the 1951 World Series, I shared the radio booth with Jim Britt, of Boston. While I was on the air, he passed me an interesting statistic he had just looked up.

"Well, now," I said, "Jim Britt just dug up another *gem* out of the record book—" and a whack right on the top of my head stopped me cold. I looked around, and there was Ed Wilhelm, the account executive for Gillette, which sponsored the Series. It was only then that I realized I had inadvertently mentioned their biggest competitor.

When Lohrke was with the Giants, everybody called him "Lucky," but we had to be careful to call him "Jack" because our sponsors were Liggett & Myers, makers of Chesterfields. For the same reason, we were never allowed to mention Camelback Mountain, which overlooks Phoenix.

We once had a promotion which called for me to say, "This is Russ Hodges talking to Joe Dokes at his store in the Bronx. Joe, what's your most popular brand of cigarettes?" Naturally, he'd say, "Chesterfields." We'd get a big backlog of interviews like that and use them for commercials between innings.

The campaign worked so well they decided to try it in Philadelphia. They hired a fine young announcer, who got several interviews on tape which were sent to New York for approval by the brass. The first thing they heard was, "This is Bill Campbell—" and that was the end of the Philadelphia experiment. It sounded too much like "Camel."

Chrysler was one of the sponsors of the 1962 World Series, which Mel Allen and I televised together, and they must have gone nuts because we were always talking about Whitey *Ford* or Jack San*ford* or Bill Staf*ford*. They just had to grin and bear it, of course. We could change Lucky Lohrke's first name but last names left us helpless.

I've never known how a commercial should be read, and there are times when I think the experts don't either. Some years ago, a well-known research outfit got evidence that there were less harmful ingredients in Chesterfields than in any other cigarette, and the advertising agency decided to break the news while we were broadcasting a Giants-Dodgers game at Ebbets Field.

On the morning of the game, an executive of the agency sent for me and said, "Russ, this is a very important announcement. It's going to kick off a nationwide campaign and will be the theme of our coast-to-coast advertising." He showed me the announcement they had prepared and said, "This can be given only one way. Read it with great care and, above all, don't preach it."

"O.K.," I said. "I won't preach it."

On the way out, another executive beckoned to me, and I stopped by at his office. He also had a copy of the announcement, which he handed to me. "Let me hear you read this nice and slowly, Russ," he said.

So I read it nice and slowly, and when I had finished, he said, "Remember, Russ, you have to be completely sincere.

The best advice I can give you is to preach it—really preach it."

"O.K.," I said. "I'll preach it."

I ended up reading it just the way I read any other announcement. I didn't hear any squawks, so I guess they were both happy.

I've never won a commercial audition in my life. When I first worked at WCKY there were three announcers, and I always ran third. When I reached network stations, if we had ten announcers, I ran tenth. I wasn't interested in the auditions. All I cared about were the jobs.

Up to 1950 I had been doing boxing for Ballantine. When Pabst Blue Ribbon took over sponsorship of the Wednesday night fights, I was out. About six months later, after the baseball season was over, I got a call from Bill Warwick, radio and television director of the agency that handled Pabst at the time.

"Would you like to do a fight for us next week?" he said.

"Sure," I said.

"Do you have any tapes of fights you've done before?" he said.

"I never save anything like that," I said.

"Well, Russ," he said, "you've got the job anyhow. I've just listened to 188 tapes of other announcers and if you can breathe you can do better."

So I was hired, and had the job seven years.

Whenever the big agencies work out a commercial, it usually has to be done over and over before they're satisfied. In 1962 we once had three new commercials to do for the Standard Oil Company of California, and the agency had us do it eighty-seven times before they found three they thought their client would accept. As far as I could see, the first three were just as good as the last.

One of my favorite brass hats among sponsors is Jim Folger, the president of Folger's Coffee. The ad agency dreamed up the idea of his doing his own commercials, and he's just enough of a ham to love it. Every so often, he gets together with us to do ten announcements at a time. He sits down, does the ten, stands up, and says, "O.K., boys. That's it." If he double-talks or flubs a word, he figures that makes him more human, and I'm sure he's right, judging by the amount of coffee he sells.

Our commercial activities do not go unnoticed. When we shifted from Falstaff Beer to Chevron Gasoline in 1962, Prescott Sullivan of the San Francisco *Examiner* wrote:

"Willie McCovey's switchover from first base to the outfield is not the only transitional experiment being undertaken at the Giants training camp in Phoenix. Of possibly even greater public interest is the reassignment of Russ Hodges and Lon Simmons from beer to oil. Owing to a change in broadcast sponsors, the club's two staff announcers are faced with the necessity of mastering a brand new line of commercials if they are to remain with the team.

"It won't be easy. Hodges and Simmons have been plugging beer on the radio for so long it has become a part of them. Now they are required to go to oil, which no one can drink. When they had a beer sponsor there was nothing that could possibly happen in a baseball game that didn't instantly remind them that it was time to go to the refrigerator for another nice, cold bottle. Will these same happenings on the ball field now remind them that it is time to dash down to the service station for a nice, cool lubrication job?"

One of the most successful commercials we had in 1962 was a bloop. Roos-Atkins, a clothing firm with stores in San Francisco and twenty-one other northern California cities, is one of our sponsors during doubleheaders. One day somebody handed us the commercial, and I started to read it. The first line said something like, "Don't be a swivel-chair scruncher." It broke me up completely.

Lon looked over my shoulder, saw the line about swivel-chair scrunchers, and he fell apart, too. We both ended up laughing our way through a commercial in which practically nothing was understandable except the name Roos-Atkins. They happened to tape it just the way we did it, and they used it several times later.

The Giants did so well in 1959 that they nearly got me into trouble with our sponsors. All sponsors have officers, agencies, and friends who want to see the World Series, and for a while it looked as if it might be played in Seals Stadium. If we had made it, I'd have had to skip town, because you couldn't put any more people into Seals Stadium for a World Series than for any other kind of a series, and everyone was after me for tickets. For a while I wouldn't even answer the telephone.

I don't think anybody dreamed we had a chance before the season began. Our rookies had looked great in 1958 and there were more coming up, but we were still short of pitchers. To bolster up that department, we got Jack Sanford from the Phillies and Sad Sam Jones from the Cardinals. We might have won the pennant, but Sanford got hit on the pitching hand in Pittsburgh and was out for five weeks. He won fifteen games as it was.

Jones had an amazing year. He won twenty-one games, and was robbed of two no-hitters, one by a Los Angeles sportswriter and the other by the weather. In the Coliseum one night in June, he hadn't allowed a hit when with one out in the eighth inning, Junior Gilliam of the Dodgers hit a soft bounding ball to shortstop. Andre Rodgers picked it up, dropped it, and picked it up again, and by then Gilliam was on first.

Charlie Park, of the Los Angeles *Mirror-News,* the official scorer, called it a hit, and not only refused to change it, but later wrote a piece called, "I Did It, Mom, and I'm Glad." I think everyone else in the ball park, including Rodgers himself, thought it was an error. I talked to all the San Francisco writers in the post-game show, and every one of them said that was the way he would have called it. When I talked to Park, he said, "Once you've called it, you can't reverse yourself."

I pointed out that John Drebinger of the New York *Times* reversed himself to give Virgil Trucks of the Tigers a no-hitter at Yankee Stadium in 1952, and that other scorers have reversed themselves when they found out they were wrong, but Park refused to change his decision.

Near the end of the season Sad Sam had another no-hitter going, this time against the Cardinals in St. Louis. They couldn't touch him for seven innings. When the Giants came up for their half of the eighth, a tremendous storm broke and the game had to be called off.

"I guess," Jones told me, "I'm going to have to settle for just one of those things." In 1955, when he was with the Cubs, he had pitched a no-hitter against the Pirates.

Jones loved Rigney, and pitched his heart out for him. On the day after Sam beat the Dodgers at the Coliseum one time, he walked up to Rig when I was about to interview Bill on the air and said, "I can give you an inning or two if you need it today." Rig did need it, and Jones saved the ball game. Afterwards, Bob Stevens of the *Chronicle* asked him if he had ever relieved before and Sam said no.

"Why not?" Bob said.

"Nobody asked me," Sam said.

He kept a supply of toothpicks, and was always chewing on one because he said it relaxed him. When he pitched his no-hitter at Chicago, Harry Creighton, one of the announcers there, gave him a gold toothpick.

Johnny Antonelli started out well in 1959, and was going along fine until early September. He won his nineteenth game on the fifth of the month but, with more than three weeks left, couldn't make it twenty. Poor Johnny was also the victim of his own fiery temper, for he pulled a rock in May that the writers and the fans of San Francisco would never let him forget.

One day we were leading the Dodgers, 2–1, at Seals Stadium behind Antonelli when Charlie Neal hit what appeared to be a routine fly ball to left field. There were some very peculiar wind currents in that ball park. They sometimes formed a sort of jet stream, and if a ball ever got into it, it was gone. That's just what happened to Neal's hit. It was carried into the bleachers for a home run and we lost the ball game.

In the locker room afterwards, Antonelli blew his stack. "This blankety-blank ball park," he raged. "How can you pitch in a lousy little joint like this?" He threw his glove across the room and stomped around, letting off steam, then disappeared into the showers.

He might have been forgiven anywhere else, but not there. He said nothing about the city, only the ball park, but in San Francisco you don't criticize anything without insulting somebody. It was a case of love me, love my ball park. The newspapers blew up Johnny's remarks all out of proportion to their importance, and one paper even editorialized that if he didn't like San Francisco, why didn't he go back where he came from?

The 1959 season was also the year of Willie McCovey's

spectacular big league debut, which came in late July. Willie was batting .372 and had already hit twenty-nine home runs in Phoenix when the Giants sent for him. We had just lost four in a row, were in the thick of the pennant race, and our hitting had slackened off. Rig was so eager to get McCovey, who was a first baseman, that he shifted Cepeda to third base and then to the outfield to make room for him.

On McCovey's first day in a Giants' uniform, he collected two triples and two singles in four trips against Robin Roberts of the Phillies, sparking us to a 7–2 victory. The next day, he singled in the eighth to drive Willie Mays home with the winning run against Pittsburgh. The day after that, he had two doubles and a single, and he hit a home run on the following day.

The Giants won six of the first seven games McCovey played in, during which time he collected five singles, two doubles, two triples, and three home runs, and was the talk of baseball. He ended up with thirteen homers and a .354 batting average in less than half a season, and was everybody's choice as Rookie of the Year.

We went into first place soon after the All-Star Game and, except for two days, remained there for ten weeks. At one point, we were four in front of the pack, and as the race moved into September, the pennant talk around San Francisco was based on more than wild hopes. We were still on top, so the other contending clubs, the Dodgers and the Braves, had to catch us.

One day I asked Rig if he thought we could hold on.

"My heart tells me yes," he said, "but my head tells me no. Let's face it, Russ. We just don't have the pitching to go all the way."

He was right. All our troubles in the last few days of the season were on the mound.

The turning point came eight days before the end, when the Dodgers beat us twice in a twinight doubleheader at Seals Stadium to pull into a top tie with us. The Braves, who also won that day, were only half a game behind. When the Dodgers beat us and Milwaukee won again the next day, we dropped to third place, half a game behind the Braves and one behind L.A. We never climbed back up.

We had one very slim chance on the last day of the season. At that point, the Braves and Dodgers were in a top tie and we were a game and a half behind, with a doubleheader to play in St. Louis. If we won both games while the other two lost their single games, there would have been a triple tie for the pennant.

Only we didn't. We dropped both games, and ended up three off the pace. Milwaukee and Los Angeles both won, forcing a playoff which the Dodgers won.

I'm never happy when we lose, but I reserve the right to breathe a sigh of relief once in a while. Seals Stadium wasn't big enough to take care of all the obligations I would have had if the Giants had won the pennant that year. With no tickets to worry about, I could answer the telephone and go to the front door again.

Each cloud has its own little silver lining. That was mine.

Chapter 15

Everybody in my business has a favorite expression, and sometimes it catches on beyond his wildest dreams. That's what happened to Mel Allen's "How about that?" which has become part of the American language. Whenever somebody on the Giants hits a home run, I say, "Bye bye baby," and our fans have picked it up and made it their own. It's a battle cry which any western follower of the Giants instantly recognizes, and we now even have a song based on it.

This melody, which was conceived one day in 1962 by Aaron Edwards, a popular KSFO announcer, is hardly a classic in the mold of "On Wisconsin" or "The Washington Post March," but it doesn't sound bad when it's played loudly enough and it's easy to sing. People at the ball park get plenty of chance to sing it because whenever something good happens to the club, Lloyd Fox belts it out on the organ weekdays while Del Courtney and his band play it on Sundays.

I'd been using the term "Bye bye baby" for home runs since 1954, but New Yorkers never adopted it. To them, it was just another pet expression by a sports announcer, such as many of us have. Mel Allen calls a home run by saying, "It's going—going—gone." Harry Caray in St. Louis says, "It might be—it could be—it *is* a home run." Curt Gowdy in Boston says, "See ya later," and Vince Scully in Los Angeles starts describing the length of the drive, then says, "Forget it, it's gone."

So it wasn't I who made "Bye bye baby" famous on the

West Coast, but the fans of San Francisco. I had always called every home run that way, whether hit by one of the Giants or somebody on the other team. When I came to San Francisco, I assumed I'd just keep right on doing it.

The first home run on opening day in 1958 was hit by Daryl Spencer in the fourth inning. As it went into the stands, I said, "Bye bye baby," just as I always had in New York. Orlando Cepeda hit one in the fifth, and I said it again. I didn't think much about it either time.

The next day, Duke Snider of the Dodgers came up in the third inning and belted a tremendous shot over the right-field fence which veteran observers said was the longest home run ever hit in Seals Stadium. The minute it left the bat we all knew it was gone, and I yelled, "Bye bye baby." A little later, Dick Gray hit one for the Dodgers, so I said it once more.

Before the game was over, we began getting phone calls from fans objecting to my using "Bye bye baby" in describing Dodgers' homers. When I stopped in at the studio later, I found out that people had been calling up all afternoon about it, and the next day we had an absolute flood of letters.

"If you're going to say 'Bye bye baby' at all," a woman wrote from Marin County, "use it just for our side. We don't want to hear it when somebody else hits one."

Her letter was typical of the hundreds that came in. So when I went to the ball park that day, I saw my duty and I did it. Gino Cimoli of the Dodgers hit one out of the park in the second inning and I simply called it a home run. But when Bob Schmidt of the Giants banged one in the fourth, I gleefully howled, "Bye bye baby." I guess everybody was happy, because the mail was predominantly favorable.

Of course "Bye bye baby" is a pretty cornball term, and not everybody liked it. For some time there was a good deal of controversy. A few newspaper columnists and fans took exception to my constant use of it, so we finally decided to see if the expression were really as popular as we thought. We ran a contest offering prizes for the best two letters of fifty words or less on two diametrically opposite subjects. One was: "I like 'Bye bye baby' because—." The other was: "I don't like 'Bye bye baby' because—."

I mentioned the contest on the air only twice, and we got 1652 letters within a few days. Of these, 1554 were for "Bye bye baby" and 98 against. That was enough to convince us, and I kept right on using it. As far as I can figure, the only ones against it today either aren't Giants' fans or just don't like pure corn. But I'm sure the vast majority of our fans are with it.

I've since been told that thousands of housewives on our network keep their radios on softly during ball games while they're working, and depend on my yell of "Bye bye baby" to let them know something special has happened. Then they drop everything, turn up the volume, find out what it was, turn the volume down again, and go back to whatever they had been doing.

We seem to have many more women fans in San Francisco than we had in New York. They come to the ball park dressed in orange and black, the Giants' colors, and they yell louder than the men. They also telephone and write much more than in New York, and they talk baseball with as much know-how and interest as any fans I've ever seen.

There isn't anyone in San Francisco quite like Hilda Chester and her cowbell, but we have a United Air Lines reservation clerk named Mrs. Ida Fish Holland who loves the Giants just as much as Hilda ever did. Normally a level-headed young lady, she gets positively bug-eyed about the ball club. She had a doll dressed in a Dodgers' uniform with the number 53 on the back. That was Don Drysdale's number, and whenever he pitched against us, Ida sat in the stands sticking pins into the doll. Drysdale failed to go the distance four times in a row.

One big difference between Giants' fans in San Francisco and New York is their average age. During our last few years in the East, most of the people who went to the Polo Grounds were middle-aged and older—fans who had been following the ball club thirty or forty years. But in Seals Stadium and later Candlestick Park, we had thousands of young married couples who often brought their babies with them. And we have always had many more youngsters at games in San Francisco than during the team's dying days in New York.

But the San Francisco Giants have yet to build a rapport with any college that compares to the emotional bond that was supposed to exist between the New York Giants and Columbia University. This may or may not have been pure fantasy, although I've run into a lot of people who claim it actually existed.

I must admit that every Columbia man I ever knew was a Giants' fan and I never even heard of one who had any use for the Yankees or the Dodgers. There must have been some sort of a link based, perhaps, on the fact that both the Columbia campus and the Polo Grounds were in Manhattan. Possibly age was a factor, too. Columbia, founded in 1754, was the oldest university in New York, and the Giants, founded in 1883, the oldest big-league baseball team there.

Eddie Brannick thinks the reason goes back to the early 1900's, when the Giants played exhibition games with the Columbia varsity, at which the college boys got to know the ballplayers. He also feels that the close friendship between Andy Coakley, the Columbia coach (who, inciden-

tally, played for the Philadelphia Athletics) and John Mc-
Graw had something to do with it.

But Columbia's Giants' fans, if there were many, were con-
spicuous by their absence during our last years in New York.
It was only when we returned for regular-season games
with the Mets and the World Series with the Yankees in 1962
that they flocked out again. From what I can gather from my
Columbia friends, our move to the West Coast hasn't dulled
their interest. They're still Giants' fans.

San Francisco's pride in its team extends to its ball park
as well. To the rest of the baseball world, Candlestick Park
is a wind tunnel where pop flies wiggle all over the place
and home runs get blown back on the field. This unhappy
idea stems from the nationally televised All-Star Game of
1961, when it was so windy that uniforms were plastered
against bodies and Stu Miller once was actually blown off
the mound.

On that same afternoon, a friend passed me a chopped
liver sandwich which, to my horror, blew out of my hand
and splattered all over a guy's face fifteen rows away. I
wasn't terribly worried about the guy—I just happen to love
chopped liver.

Believe me—and I'm afraid many of my friends don't—
that was the windiest day I ever saw at Candlestick Park.
We do have a wind that is a bit unusual, but it's nowhere
nearly as bad as the jet stream at Seals Stadium. There's
always a breeze blowing inside the park which tangles with
the prevailing wind from the west when it hits, with the
result that there's some swirling of dust for fifteen or twenty
minutes. When the prevailing wind finally does take over,
however, there's no problem.

Players and managers allow for this wind in San Francisco, just as they allow for local conditions in every big-

league ball park. Our wind blows toward right field, so fielders are positioned and pitchers instructed accordingly. The fielders play deep and close to the right-field foul line. Pitchers try to keep the ball away from left-handed batters and close to right-handers so they are more likely to hit to left. This is not much different, for example, from the instructions every pitcher gets at Yankee Stadium, where the right-field stands are within fairly easy reach and it's a long drive to left.

Candlestick Point was a perfect place for a ball park. For a while there had been talk of building one in San Mateo County, south of the city, not far from Bay Meadows race track. That idea died because it was beyond the city limits. Another group thought of condemning some building in a blighted downtown area, but that wouldn't have been practical. There was even talk of double-decking Seals Stadium, but that would simply have complicated an already serious parking problem.

Candlestick Point was finally chosen because it was within the city limits, could be constructed without depriving people of their homes, and was easily accessible via a super-highway from both north and south. I first saw the site when we televised a show from there in 1958. Later, we did progress reports on TV while the park was being built.

It was ready for the opening of the 1960 season. We were still trying to bolster our pitching staff, and had acquired Billy O'Dell from Baltimore in a midwinter trade. Precisely what happened to our ball club that year is something none of us can figure out. We looked strong and a lot of experts thought we'd win the pennant.

We started out as if we would. With a crowd of over forty-one thousand on hand to help us unveil the new park, Sam Jones pitched a three-hit shutout victory over the Cardinals on opening day. In early May, we swept three straight from the Pirates, and went on to win four more games in a row to go into first place. We moved back and forth between first and second for several weeks, but something was wrong. We all seemed to sense that it wouldn't last.

In early June we went into a nosedive, losing eight out of eleven, and that was the end of our pennant hopes. In the meantime, there had been rumors that Bill Rigney was through, but they couldn't be confirmed.

Rig and I were doing a radio show twice a week from the ball park. One day, just before we went on the air, he said, "Well, Russ, I'm still here, but I don't know whether I'll be here or not next week."

A few days later, he was leaning against the batting cage before a ball game, and Chub Feeney walked over to him. Before Chub said a word, Rig said, "I guess you're going to tell me something, and I don't think I'm going to like it."

"I'm sorry, Rig," Chub said, "but I'm afraid you're right. This is it. You're being replaced."

"O.K.," Rig said. "I've had four and a half wonderful years with the Giants, and that's something I'll always remember."

So he went into the clubhouse, took off his uniform, said goodbye to the ballplayers, and watched the game from the press box. We all wished him the best, and were delighted when he did so well with the Los Angeles Angels in 1962.

Rigney's successor was Tom Sheehan, a veteran scout who was obviously an interim appointment. At the time, none of us knew whom Horace Stoneham had in mind for permanent manager, but we suspected it was an active ballplayer on another club who wouldn't be available until the season was over. However, there was a great deal of speculation about Leo Durocher.

It started in New York, and was so persistent that San

Francisco writers couldn't ignore it. As far as any of us knew, Durocher and Horace Stoneham didn't even meet during that period, but stories were repeatedly printed to the effect that they were in constant touch with each other and that Leo's appointment was imminent. The fact that his television contract was due to expire at the end of the year intensified the rumors.

One day about a month after Rig left, the Durocher story became so hot that every paper in town declared he would sign a contract momentarily. At the time, Stoneham was just returning from a league meeting in Chicago. As soon as he got home he called a press conference to straighten the matter out.

"There seems to be a definite newspaper campaign on in New York to install Durocher as our manager, and it's getting a little embarrassing," he said. "Nothing will be done at this time. And Durocher definitely will not manage the Giants."

It was the only way Stoneham could end all the gossip. It was attracting more attention than the ball club, which wasn't doing very well. The team had long since dropped out of contention, for nothing went right on the field.

Willie McCovey started the season like the second coming of Willie Mays, hitting seven home runs in his first fifteen games. After that he folded, and his batting average dropped all the way to .244. First Rigney, then Sheehan tried everything to get him to start hitting again. He even went to Tacoma for a couple of weeks to see if he could sharpen his eye on minor league pitching. It helped some, but not very much.

But McCovey wasn't our only problem. The infield didn't click, especially in the last half of the season. What should have been a good second-base combination of Don Blasingame at second and Eddie Bressoud at short didn't work out too well. Both later starred elsewhere, but neither was a howling success at Candlestick Park.

The pitching staff started out all right and then died. By midseason the only men we could depend on were Sam Jones, who won eighteen games, and Mike McCormick, whose 2.70 earned-run average was the best in the league. Johnny Antonelli, still the target of the fans' scorn because of his blowup over the Seals Stadium wind the year before, had a bad season. So did Billy O'Dell, who won eight and lost thirteen.

There were a few bright spots. Juan Marichal, a twenty-one-year-old right-hander from the Dominican Republic, came down from Tacoma in July and pitched a one-hitter against the Phils. Only Clay Dalrymple's single with two out in the eighth inning stopped him from landing in the Hall of Fame on his first try. Marichal finished the season with six wins and two losses.

Orlando Cepeda reached his prime and, with Willie Mays, gave the Giants the best one-two punch in the National League. Cepeda hit twenty-four home runs, drove in ninety-six runs, and had a .297 batting average. Willie finished up with twenty-nine homers, 103 RBI's, and a .319 average, the third best in the league. But Cepeda remained the darling of the fans. They still weren't ready to forgive Mays for his great years at the Polo Grounds. They would accept him as one of their own eventually, but not yet.

We finished fifth, and no one was happier than Tom Sheehan to see the season end. A jolly, friendly man with a wonderful disposition and an inexhaustible supply of funny stories, he never wanted the manager's job and accepted it only as a favor to Stoneham. Once in a while, the boys took advantage of his good nature, but Tom rarely got upset.

Whenever he wanted to remove a pitcher—and the occasion arose often that year—Tom always walked to the mound with his head down. One day in Milwaukee, Jack Sanford was having a rough time, and Sheehan decided to take him out. He stepped from the dugout and, staring at his feet, slowly started for the pitcher's box. Sanford saw him coming, dropped the ball, and headed rapidly for the bench, passing Tom on the way.

The place exploded when Sheehan looked up finally and discovered that he was the last person in the ball park to know he had no pitcher to yank. That one cost Sanford a few bucks, a disciplinary fine that he probably figured was worth its weight in laughs.

We had a few in the radio booth, too, where life is so confusing that the place is popularly known as the "boar's nest." Chub Feeney, the Giants' vice president and one of the most superstitious men I know, likes to sit there because he thinks it's good luck. At the Polo Grounds, where there was no barrier between the booth and the press box, Chub used to pace back and forth, but ended up with us. At Seals Stadium the booth was barely big enough for the broadcasting personnel. But Candlestick Park has a spacious booth with room for one and all, including Feeney and anyone who cares to visit him during the ball game.

The engineers sit up in the back row, worrying what's going to happen next, and they have plenty to worry about. Feeney sits in a far corner of the front row, poised to blow his stack as he glowers at the ballplayers. His telephone is almost never still, and he bellows into it as though whoever is on the other end were stone deaf. So, always in the background—when we can keep it there—is Chub's end of a conversation, which can be anything from an argument over a trade to a discourse on why he can't deliver six tickets beside the Giants' dugout on the spot.

No matter how busy he is, Feeney misses nothing on the field, or any opportunity to comment thereupon. One day, the pitcher made a great stop, picked up the ball, and threw it to second base. Before I could say a word into the microphone, Chub roared, "Third base—throw it to third, you stupid blankety-blank."

That line bounced off the ears of Giants' fans from Phoenix to Honolulu and from Eureka to Salinas, while Lon, our engineers, and I cringed.

Fortunately, we have a cutoff button which both Lon and I have become adept at using. We reach for it automatically when something happens which we know will result in a Feeney explosion. One day, when a promising Giants' rally was killed by a double play, I cut the mike and waited for the inevitable, but nothing happened. After a minute or so, I figured nothing would, so I released the button. At that moment, Feeney slammed his fist on the table, causing the microphone to bounce up and hit me on the chin. It nearly knocked me cold, and I can't imagine what it sounded like to our long-suffering listeners.

The press box is on the other side of a window to our right, so newspapermen are always coming in to see Feeney. They get into discussions that start on a low key, with Chub piously warning, "Not too loud—we don't want to bother Russ." But sooner or later, they erupt into a heated argument over the merits of a ballplayer or a controversial play, and I have to cut the mike and plaintively plead, "Gentlemen—for the love of Mike—*shut up*." They quiet right down, but pretty soon they're at it again. Between us, Lon and I press our panic button half a dozen times during a game.

When Chub is quiet, we have to contend with Franklin Mieuli, who sits in the other corner. Franklin is not only our producer, but is also connected with the 49ers football team and the Warriors basketball team. He can watch a baseball game and talk football or basketball without missing a play, and he has as many people to talk to as Feeney. Like Chub, Franklin starts out whispering, while cautioning his visitors to be careful not to bother Russ or Lon, but his discussions increase in volume as they go along, and pretty soon whichever one of us is on the air has to push the button and yell for silence.

We must have the busiest radio booth in the big leagues. People not only come in to see Chub or Franklin, but to get somebody's autograph, or to say hello, or to use a telephone, or to keep warm, or just to visit.

So sometimes our broadcasts don't make much sense, but we get by. And I've become so used to the boar's nest that peace and quiet scare me. I like confusion better.

Chapter 16

The news that Alvin Dark was our new manager caught me by surprise. I didn't have any idea the job was his until I saw him standing beside Chub Feeney at a press conference about a month after the disastrous 1960 season ended. When I thought about it later, I couldn't understand how I had missed Dark as a prime candidate. He satisfied all of Stoneham's requirements for a manager. He had been a fine, aggressive ballplayer and a natural leader, and he was a former Giant from a highly successful era. On top of that, he was a decent, clean-cut, deeply religious young man of great character who would be a credit to the ball club.

During the course of his active career he had wandered all over the National League. We got him from Boston and traded him to St. Louis. After that, he had played in Chicago, Philadelphia, and finally Milwaukee. He came to San Francisco in a straight player swap for Andre Rodgers, and his appointment as manager was announced the next day.

There were the usual introductions and interviews and palaver, during which we all asked the obvious questions and got the obvious answers. (Sample question: "Do you think the Giants will win the pennant?" Sample answer: "We'll do the best we can.") This went on for three hours, during which Alvin impressed us all with his patience and sincerity. He said the same things over and over without getting annoyed, and everyone went away satisfied. He made a deep impression on us all.

But the payoff is on the field, of course, and I was eager

to see Dark in action. I didn't have to wait long before learning that Alvin was different from any other manager I had ever watched. At spring training in Phoenix, he handled pitchers in a way all his own.

At our first intrasquad game, I said, "How long will the pitchers work?"

"About fifty pitches," he said.

"I mean—how many innings?" I said.

"And I mean about fifty pitches," Alvin said. "If a man is wild or in trouble, he may not last one inning. If he's going well, he may last five."

Dark's first move at Candlestick Park was to reverse the bullpens. Ours had been in the right-field corner, adjacent to the clubhouse, where a weary, cold, or bored ballplayer could duck inside for coffee or a smoke if the spirit moved him. It was impossible to see it from our dugout behind first base because of the angle. Alvin changed our pitchers to the left-field bullpen. There, the boys have nothing to do but watch the ball game, because there's nowhere else to go. Just to make sure they're paying attention, Alvin can now keep an eye on them from his place on the bench.

The 1961 season was a shakedown year, so there were several trades, and Dark did a lot of experimenting. In December of 1960, we sent Antonelli and Kirkland to Cleveland for Harvey Kuenn, a great hitter who could play equally well in the infield or the outfield. And right after the season began, we got Ed Bailey from the Reds for Don Blasingame, Bob Schmidt, and Roadblock Jones, a pitcher.

A former shortstop himself, Alvin was deeply impressed by little José Pagan, who had come to us from Tacoma near the end of the 1960 season. Before the year was over, Pagan was our regular shortstop, and Bressoud was expendable. He went to Houston at the end of the season, from where he was traded to the Red Sox. Dark also closely watched the progress of Tom Haller and Chuck Hiller at Tacoma. Haller was a fine catcher, but big-league pitching mystified him. Hiller was a promising second baseman, who wasn't quite ready for the majors. Both had been up with the Giants and were getting valuable experience in the Pacific Coast League.

Dark, ordinarily mild-mannered, has a surprisingly hot temper. One day in midseason, after a bad game in Philadelphia, Alvin stalked into the clubhouse, picked up a stool, and tried to throw it across the room. But a nail sticking out of it ripped off the tip of one of Dark's little fingers, so Alvin had to go to the hospital for repairs.

When Manager Fred Hutchinson of the Reds, an old hand at throwing things across locker rooms, heard about it, he said, "Alvin shouldn't try that. He hasn't had enough practice."

Dark is a master of the soft sell. He rarely raises his voice, never swears, never badgers, and never criticizes a ballplayer in the presence of others. He treats each man as an individual, and has a sixth sense in the handling of human problems. He's strict without being a martinet and considerate without being an easy mark. As a result, he quickly won everyone's respect and confidence, and even had some ballplayers helping him do his own job.

For example, one day early in the 1961 season, a rookie failed to run out a ground ball. Harvey Kuenn, a veteran who had just joined the ball club, pulled him aside later and said, "I don't care what you're doing to yourself, but I don't like what you're doing to Alvin."

The rookie never loafed again.

Dark is a deep thinker, always a jump or two ahead of everyone else. He sometimes uses what appears to be weird strategy, but it's wise to talk to him before second-guessing him. He never does anything without a good reason, and he's always willing to explain.

One day in Chicago he made a series of moves so mystifying that we thought he had popped his cork. With the game tied 2–2 and one out in the last of the ninth, the Cubs had a man on second and Ernie Banks at bat. Bob Bolin, a right-hander, was pitching for us and, with first base open, it was obvious that Dark wanted Banks intentionally passed.

Alvin picked that moment to take Bolin out, replacing him with the left-handed Billy O'Dell. At the same time, he yanked Hiller, a weak hitter but our best-fielding second baseman, and sent in Joey Amalfitano, who couldn't field with Hiller but was a much better hitter. O'Dell then walked Banks intentionally, bringing up the left-handed George Altman. When the Cubs sent the right-handed George Freese up to bat for Altman, Dark yanked O'Dell for the right-handed Sam Jones. The Cubs promptly pulled out Freese and sent the left-handed Bob Will to the plate. Will grounded out, and Jones eventually got out of the inning. We finally won the game in the thirteenth.

All of us upstairs were puzzled by the same things. Why did Dark waste O'Dell, using him only to issue an intentional pass, which Bolin could have done just as well? And why did Dark yank Hiller when he did? Wouldn't it have made more sense to keep the better fielder in the game while the Cubs were still batting and save the better hitter for when we came up?

When Charlie Einstein, then covering the club for the San Francisco *Examiner*, asked Dark those questions, Alvin's answers were completely logical, and typical of the way his mind runs.

The rules say a new pitcher must face at least one batter

before he can be taken out. This doesn't apply to a pinch-hitter. He can be yanked without stepping into the batter's box. Dark wanted Jones to pitch, but didn't want him facing the dangerous Altman. He figured that the Cubs, thinking O'Dell would stay in the game, would send Freese up to bat for Altman, which they did. Dark, not wanting O'Dell to pitch to Freese, could now yank O'Dell, since he had already pitched to Banks. Dark knew the Cubs wouldn't let Freese face Jones, but would send another left-hander to the plate. The best one they had on the bench was Will, a far weaker batter than Altman, the original hitter in that slot, and Dark didn't mind Jones' facing him.

So, by sending O'Dell out on what seemed a useless errand in a tough situation, Dark made the Cubs waste their three best clutch hitters, Banks, Altman, and Freese. Not one was permitted a single swing of his bat and two were finessed right out of the game.

What about the Amalfitano substitution for Hiller? Simple, my dear Watson. The pitcher was due to come up ahead of Hiller. By putting Amalfitano into the game when he did, Dark could juggle his batting order around by inserting Amalfitano in the pitcher's slot and using Jones where Hiller had been batting. If the game lasted long enough, Amalfitano would get an extra time at bat. That was just what did happen, and Amalfitano eventually scored the winning run.

Dark is also a psychologist of no mean ability. When few of our starting pitchers went the distance during the first half of the season, he decided to do something about it. One hot night in Pittsburgh in late July, he told me that he wasn't going to use his bullpen. Then he handed Marichal the ball and said, "Juan, do you think you can go nine?"

"I'll try," Marichal said.

"That's not enough," Dark said. "You're going nine, no matter what happens."

The bullpen was empty that night. Marichal, with no relief to lean on, went the distance for the first time in six weeks, and shut out the Pirates, 2–0.

Two nights later, in Philadelphia, Dark said to Mike McCormick, who had completed only three games in six weeks, "You're going nine tonight."

The dugouts in Philadelphia are too small to take care of the whole squad, so there were men in our bullpen that night, but none of them worked. McCormick got into several tight situations, survived them all, and won a 4–3 victory all by himself.

The next night Dark tossed the ball to Sanford, who had completed two games all year.

"I know," Sanford said. "I'm going nine."

"That's right," said Alvin. "Good luck."

The Phillies filled the bases with none out in the seventh inning. With a 5–2 lead, Sanford glanced toward the bullpen, but everybody there, including Stu Miller, our ace relief pitcher, was sitting down. Jack turned back to his job, kept the Phillies from scoring, and went on to win the ball game.

Two days after that, Marichal pitched a one-hitter in Los Angeles to win his second straight shutout—and he went all the way.

Bob Stevens of the *Chronicle* asked Dark how much longer he thought the Giants could go without a bullpen. Alvin smiled and said, "Of course I'll go to the bullpen if necessary. All I've tried to do is prove to these fellows that they can go nine innings if they have to. They were just getting too dependent on Stu Miller."

Dark had some other unusual ideas. He thought slow men sometimes had a better chance to steal than speed demons, on the theory that the opposition would be caught by surprise. He proved it with Harvey Kuenn, who rarely stole in previous years. Kuenn stole five bases in 1961, practically all in key situations.

Alvin also felt that ball clubs didn't bunt often enough. He used the sacrifice and the squeeze play more often than any manager I've ever seen. He didn't always get away with it, with the result that the Giants sometimes looked a little silly.

One night Cepeda, a power hitter, was twice ordered to bunt, failed both times, then struck out. Asked about it later, Dark said, "In each case I felt the bunt was called for. If either had been successful, we might have won the game."

Several times Dark resorted to the colorful suicide squeeze, which is great when it works but horrible when it doesn't. In the suicide squeeze, the runner starts from third base with the pitch and doesn't stop. The batter must bunt, or at least get a piece of the ball. If he misses, the runner is a dead duck. We lost a ball game one night because the opposing catcher ordered a pitchout which the hitter couldn't have reached with a ten-foot bat, and of course Dark had to take the rap for it.

"That's the chance you always take with a suicide squeeze," he said later. "But it's a great play and we'll use it any time we think we can make it work."

Another night we won a ball game when Alvin threw away the managerial book and invented one of his own. We took advantage of errors, wild pitches, and bases on balls, scrambled around with bunts in odd situations, and did all sorts of things that made sense to Alvin, but nobody else.

Later, in the press room, Curley Grieve, the *Examiner* sports editor, said, "You know, Russ, I can't figure out exactly what happened. How did we win this ball game?"

"You've got me," I said. "Maybe Alvin owns stock in a

chain of nuthouses and he's trying to fill them with guys like you and me."

"Well," Grieve said, "I'm sure of one thing. Outside of the old boy himself, Alvin is the nearest thing to Casey Stengel I've ever seen."

Dark is a devout Baptist, who has always tithed—given one-tenth of his income to the church, but in his zeal to win, he sometimes does things that worry him later. He once ordered our groundskeeper, Matty Schwab, to soak the infield before a game with the Dodgers. He wanted to slow down Maury Wills, the fabulous Los Angeles base-stealer. Seething Dodgers' fans, including many ministers and former ministers, wrote him some pretty rough letters which deeply disturbed him.

One day he showed me a fistful of them. "Maybe the next time we're in Los Angeles, I ought to go on the air with Vince Scully and try to explain my side of the situation," he said.

"Alvin," I said, "once you're convicted in the eyes of a baseball fan, there isn't a thing you can do. An apology wouldn't help. Are all the letters from southern California?"

"Yes," he said.

"Any from northern California?" I said.

"Not one," he said.

"And they're all from Baptists?" I said.

"Most of them," he said. "I guess they know I'm a Baptist."

"Alvin," I said, "I wouldn't worry about it. You're from Louisiana, but you live in northern California now. And you must know better than anyone else that a northern Baptist never pays any attention to anything a southern Baptist says."

I left with my chin intact, but I guess Alvin was satisfied. He never asked Scully to put him on the air in Los Angeles.

The Reds won the 1961 pennant, the Dodgers were second,

and we finished third. Part of our trouble was pitching. Except for Miller, the best fireman in the National League, we didn't have a man who won more than thirteen games, a figure which Marichal, McCormick, and Sanford hit on the nose. Miller won fourteen and saved twelve. Sam Jones had a mediocre 8–8 season, and nobody else helped much.

But pitching wasn't our only problem. While our one-two punch of Cepeda and Mays was tremendous and Felipe Alou did well, the rest of our hitting was disappointing. Kuenn, a former American League batting champion and a consistent .300 hitter, flopped to .265. McCovey had eighteen homers, but batted only .271, far below his potential.

Still, Dark wasn't really worried about our power. He knew it would improve in 1962. The changes he wanted were designed to improve our pitching, and in November the front office made exactly the trade that would help him the most. In the Giants' only important deal of the year, they sent Dom Zanni, Eddie Fisher, and Bob Farley to the Chicago White Sox for Billy Pierce and Don Larsen.

At spring training, Dark told me one day, "If Hiller, Pagan, and Haller do what I think they can do, and if the hitting comes back as it should, I think we now have the pitching we need to win the pennant."

Doc Bowman, the trainer, said precisely the same thing in much simpler terms. In the clubhouse at Phoenix, he posted a sign that read: "Work hard this year and eat corn on the cob all winter."

Chapter 17

Our unbelievable finish in 1962 was the climax of the daffiest season I have ever known. It was a year of birds and beasts and brawls and a silly noise that goes, roughly, "n-n-n-N-N-N-." Any Los Angeles fan will tell you that's a duck call, but it sounded to me more like a Bronx cheer.

"N-n-n-N-N-N-" would never have jarred my eardrums except for the fact that the Candlestick Park infield must be sprinkled before games because the wind might otherwise kick up dust and make conditions tough for the ballplayers. Matty Schwab, our groundskeeper, dutifully hosed it daily.

Alvin Dark's conscience notwithstanding, he never discouraged Matty from doing a particularly thorough job when the Dodgers came to town. The more water, the less speed, and the less speed, the less effective on the basepaths were Maury Wills, and Tommy and Willie Davis, the tremendously fast Los Angeles stars.

Sometimes Schwab got carried away. This happened in early August, when the Dodgers came in for their last series of the year at Candlestick Park. Half an hour before game time the infield looked like a rice paddy.

As I left the dugout to go up to the radio booth, Ron Fairly of the Dodgers yelled, "Hey, Alvin, what time does the tide come in?" And, as I walked by Duke Snider, I distinctly heard him humming "Chloe," the song about the girl who was lost in the swamp. Of course the ground was too soft for stealing, and the Dodgers' flying squadron did little.

The Giants swept the series and from then on Alvin Dark

has been known in Los Angeles as the "Swamp Fox." And when we went to L.A. for our last series there in early September, we were all greeted by "n-n-n-N-N-N-." This chorus was the product of an inspired Los Angeles duck-call vendor, who advertised his wares in the newspapers the day before the Giants arrived.

"Since the Giants are more like ducks than ballplayers," his ad said, in effect, "why not give them a taste of their own medicine? Buy a duck-call and blow it at the Giants tomorrow."

He must have sold a lot of duck-calls, because when the Giants came out to the field, Chavez Ravine sounded like Okefenokee. There were "n-n-n-N-N-N-s" to the left of them, "n-n-n-N-N-N-s" to the right of them, "n-n-n-N-N-N-s" all around them, and everybody who wasn't "n-n-n-N-N-N-ing" was laughing like crazy, including the radio crew. I thought Lon was going to fall right out of the booth.

The Giants themselves added to the chorus. Billy O'Dell and Ed Bailey, both enthusiastic duck hunters, could "n-n-n-N-N-N-" with the experts, so we decided to do something about it. The next day, I bought one of those duck-calls, and opened the pre-game show with it. Then we had a duck-calling contest, which O'Dell won hands down.

The salesman did very well, and so did the Dodgers—at the gate, that is. We beat them three out of four, but with that fabulous "n-n-n-N-N-N-" buildup, every game was a sellout. It was a clutch series, but I've never been sure how many people came out to see the ball game and how many to listen to the call of the wild.

One night that summer I looked down at the Giants' bullpen and did a double take. "Lon," I said, "am I seeing things or is that a rooster?"

"That's a rooster," he said.

But we were wrong. As we watched, the creature struck a fighting pose and charged, while the ballplayers scattered. It was a fighting cock some friendly fan had let loose. Nobody dared go near him, and they had to stop the ball game for several minutes before he could be corraled. While they were trying to catch up with him, Vince Scully remarked, "Look at the fowl in foul territory."

Another time, a gorgeous pheasant appeared, and strutted along the third-base line. He was nowhere near as difficult to catch as the fighting cock, but nobody tried to get him for a few minutes. He was such a stunning sight, preening and slowly marching back and forth like a peacock, that the fans wanted to watch him for a while. Finally, the bat boy walked out, picked him up, and carted him off the field.

But the same fellow had a terrible time with a rabbit one night. Somebody threw the animal out of the grandstand, and he scooted along the first-base line with the bat boy in hot pursuit. Lon was on the air, and he called it like a dog race, where greyhounds chase a mechanical rabbit around the track.

"There goes the rabbit," said Lon, "and there's the bat boy after him—now there's a policeman—and the first-base umpire—and a couple of ballplayers—only the numbers aren't right—"

The rabbit disappeared in the outfield, while Lon said, with a note of sadness in his voice, "Same old story—the rabbit always wins—"

One of Matty Schwab's groundskeepers, a guy named Shorty, always brought a dog around, and he's had some beauties. One night, with the Dodgers in town, Shorty showed up with a nine-months-old Dalmatian, which liked to play with everybody. The ballplayers loved him, and so did everyone else, because this was the friendliest dog you ever met.

Jerry Doggett, who works with Vince Scully on Dodgers' broadcasts, had to go down to the field to do a post-game show on television. Jerry, wearing a white trench coat, charged out to the field the minute the game ended, and the Dalmatian charged after him. Dog and man arrived together in front of the Dodgers' dugout, and the dog stole the show. He grabbed Jerry's coat, and Jerry fell just as he went on the air. He did the whole program from a prone position with Shorty's friendly Dalmatian standing over him like a sentinel.

That looked terribly funny to me, and I laughed and laughed, but I had an embarrassing moment of my own before the camera the last time we went into Los Angeles. I'm not the world's sharpest dresser. My taste runs heavily to sloppy knit sports shirts, open at the throat, and baggy pants, but I can look reasonably neat if I have to. Our Los Angeles trip was the first stop of a long eastern swing, so I had taken plenty of clothes with me. And, since we would be on television at Chavez Ravine, I had a different outfit for each of the four games we'd play there. This included four blue suits, four of those special television blue shirts which look white in your living room, and four sporty neckties.

All this was for our pre-game show when I would be on camera. Nobody with a figure like mine could ever be mistaken for a Brooks Brothers model, but at least I could look like an ad for what the well-dressed fat man should wear. My tie was in place, my hair combed, my shirt neat, and my trousers pressed. I bore this burden until the show was over, then stripped off my jacket, ripped off my tie, and tore open my shirt collar. By the time I reached the booth where I could exchange my television blue for a comfortable knit creation, I looked my usual sloppy self.

The last game of the series was a killer that carried us all away. It was a seesaw battle that lasted more than three hours and had everyone sitting on the edge of his seat. The payoff came in the ninth inning when Harvey Kuenn belted a double with the bases full, scoring three runs and giving the Giants a 9–6 victory. When it was all over, I looked as if I had just gone through a cement mixer.

This was our last scheduled appearance in Los Angeles, so I said a few words about the great Giants-Dodgers rivalry. Bill Parry, our television producer, decided that would be a great time to throw me on camera. I almost fainted when I looked at the monitor. There I was, covered with perspiration, my matted hair flopping all over my face, and my rumpled, streaked shirt open at the throat, with the collar curled up like the ends of an old french fried potato.

"All right," I said, "maybe I don't look so good. But if you've been with us all night, I'll bet you don't either. Just go take a look in the mirror and see for yourself." Then I signed off.

The Giants normally don't get into many brawls, but they had a few beauties during the early stages of the 1962 pennant race, which I think helped fuse them into a one-for-all, all-for-one unit. The first erupted at Forbes Field in Pittsburgh. Bob Friend was pitching a good game for the Pirates when somebody raked him for a home run, ruffling his feelings no end. Ed Bailey stepped to the plate, and Friend's first pitch sailed right over his head. Bailey started for the mound, but before he reached there, Don Leppert, the Pirates' catcher, was on his back.

The next thing we knew, both dugouts were boiling over, and guys were squaring off all over the place. It took several minutes to get everybody separated. Bailey finally stepped back up to the plate, and when Friend tried to slip a fast ball by him, Ed hit it high up in the right-center-field bleachers, a really tremendous blast. He ran around the bases grinning and making faces at Friend, while the boys in our dugout cheered like college kids.

Not long after that, Willie Mays got into the only fight of his career. He was on second base and Cepeda on first in a game against the New York Mets at Candlestick Park. Roger Craig, the Mets' pitcher, made several attempts to pick Mays off second base. On one of them, Willie crashed hard into Elio Chacon, the shortstop, and Chacon blew his stack.

He threw a punch at Mays, and Willie picked him up, tossed him to the ground, and fell on top of him. By that time, Cepeda had come over to join the party, and Craig had rushed off the mound to intercept him. Chub Feeney, watching almost half a million dollars worth of Giants' ballplayers rolling around in the dirt, yelled, "Break it up—break it up—" while the crowd roared.

One of the great moments of the 1962 season came in early June when we returned to the Polo Grounds for the first time in five years, to play the Mets. As we entered the ball park, I thought of that last locker room scene—of Hans Lobert's sorrow because the Giants lost, of Eddie Brannick's tears, of Buddy Kerr's attitude of resignation and of Sid Gordon's silent grief. I had thought then that there would never again be a big-league ball game in the shadow of Coogan's Bluff, but of course I was wrong.

I felt odd as I went into the visitors' radio booth, and odder still when I looked over at the Mets' booth and saw Ralph Kiner there as one of the home team announcers. I thought of that wonderful day in 1951 when Bobby Thomson hit his home run and of Bob Prince's priceless signoff: "The Giants won the pennant, but remember—Ralph Kiner is still

the home run champion of the National League—and now—
Russ Hodges—"

I looked at the crowd of more than forty-three thousand
fans and thought of the days when Bob Delaney and Jim
Woods and I had to be careful not to let our voices echo in
the silence, and I wondered why the Giants were so much
more attractive to New York fans as foes than they had been
as friends.

Then came the biggest moment of all—the introduction of
Willie Mays. As he stood near the Giants' dugout, grinning
and waving his cap, the crowd gave him an ovation that must
have lasted ten minutes. Willie obliged them all later with a
tremendous home run, and the crowd roared some more as
he trotted around the bases.

I don't know why, but I always had the feeling that that
helped as much as anything to make Willie completely accepted at last by San Francisco fans. When we got home
after that trip, they cheered him more than they ever had
before, and they were with him for the rest of the year. It
was as if everyone realized that Mays went back to New York
as a member of the *San Francisco* Giants, and that he belonged to San Francisco just as much as Cepeda or any of
the others who had never played for the New York Giants.

We led the league until the early part of July, when the
Dodgers took over. They stayed there all summer, and when
we went into L.A. for our final series in early September, they
were three and a half games in front. Mays' forty-second
homer won the first game, and that made it two and a half,
but the Dodgers won the second. However, when we took
the last two, we left town only a game and a half behind, and
were still very much alive in the pennant race.

Both teams had terrible eastern swings. A reasonable
stretch of luck would have clinched it for either club, but

the Dodgers couldn't get rolling and neither could we. We ran into a six-game losing streak, and what looked like disaster struck right in the middle of it when Willie Mays collapsed on the bench in Cincinnati. It turned out to be nothing worse than exhaustion, but he missed a game against the Reds and a whole series in Pittsburgh, and gave us all heart failure.

We looked so bad that even I almost gave up hope when we headed back west. The only thing that saved us was the fact that the Dodgers were just as bad. They didn't seem to want to win the pennant either, so they were still in sight when we got home.

When the race went down to Saturday, September 29, the next-to-last day of the season, we were still alive, but barely breathing. Because of a rainout the night before, we had to play that doubleheader against Houston in the afternoon, after which the Dodgers would play their single night game with the Cardinals at Chavez Ravine. We were a game and a half behind, so if we lost both games or even if we split and the Dodgers won, it would be all over. But if we either split or won two, that night game in Los Angeles would be very important to us. Every fan in town would want to know how it was coming out.

A couple of hours before our doubleheader started, I was munching on a cold tongue sandwich in the Curley Grieve press room at Candlestick Park when Bob Hansen phoned. He was looking for Franklin Mieuli, who hadn't yet arrived, so I took the message.

"I thought you'd like to know it's going to be a long day," Bob said. "You and Mr. Simmons and Mr. Mieuli are cordially ordered to appear in the studios of KSFO at eight o'clock tonight to do a telegraphic re-creation of the Dodgers-Cardinals game."

I gagged on the sandwich, and said, "I sort of expected that. Do we get paid?"

"Not according to the contract," Bob said.

"I sort of expected that, too," I said. "We'll be there."

The Giants won the first game, but lost the second. We were off the air at six-eighteen and arrived at the studio in the Hotel Fairmont a little after seven, giving us just enough time for a bite to eat before going back to work.

Gene D'Alessi, one of the studio's regular engineers, had everything all rigged up for us. He had spent the entire day going through our tapes of previous Dodgers' games, taking out cheers, groans, boos, organ music, applause, and even a tape of the stadium crowd singing the National Anthem. Just for insurance, in case anything went wrong with the telegraphic facilities, Monty Bancroft, from Mieuli's office, had set up a short-wave receiver and was prepared to get the radio broadcast direct from Chavez Ravine if necessary.

Lon and I squeezed into a glassed-in cubbyhole only slightly bigger than a telephone booth, where if one of us sneezed, the other would get pneumonia. Mieuli ran the copy in from the printer, while D'Alessi stood peering in at us for crowd noise cues.

"They're playing The Star-Spangled Banner," the first note read. Lon pointed to Gene and he put on the National Anthem tape. The next one said: "The Dodgers are running out on the field," and D'Alessi put on the organ playing the Dodgers' "Charge" music, interspersed with cheers and whistles from the crowd.

"Drysdale walks out to the field" (cheers)—"Javier up" (more cheers for Drysdale)—"Javier out" (cheers)—"Flood out" (cheers)—"Musial out" (cheers and a "charge").

In the meantime, I filled in all the color from scraps of information that Mieuli brought in, while Lon and I talked about the crowd, the weather, the pretty girls, and whatever else we imagined might be happening in Dodger Stadium that night.

Now it was the Cardinals' second, and we started again. "Boyer out" (cheers)—"James singles" (groans)—"Oliver out" (cheers)—"Maxville flies to right" (cheers)—*"Howard drops the ball"* (groans and boos)—"James scores, Maxville goes all the way to third" (more groans and boos)—"Broglio up" (scattered cheers)—"Broglio singles, scoring Maxville" (groans and boos again)—"Javier fans" (cheers and a half-hearted "charge").

Those two runs were the ball game. Broglio held the Dodgers to two singles, one by Snider, the other by Moon. Willie Davis and Snider each stole a base, and the Dodgers pulled off a couple of double plays, but these were about the only times D'Alessi could put on the cheers or the "charge" tape. The tape with the boos got a fair play and the one with the groans was just about worn out by the time the game was over.

The whole thing was so realistic that people asked Lon and me for weeks how we got from Candlestick Park to Chavez Ravine so fast.

The Cardinals' 2–0 victory left us only a game behind the Dodgers, and set the stage for that frenetic final day and the insanely wonderful playoffs. And when the last game of that series was over in Los Angeles, we all had to hustle back to San Francisco for the opening of the World Series against the Yankees the next day.

Everybody was pretty tired, so the trip was uneventful except for an occasional whoop here and there. My only other impression of the journey itself was of Doc Bowman repeating over and over, "Corn on the cob all winter—corn on the cob all winter—"

As usual, Lon and I had announced our approximate arrival time at the San Francisco airport, mostly for the benefit of wives and families who might want to meet the plane. We figured a few thousand fans might show up too, but we were hardly prepared for the mob scene that greeted us.

The flight from Los Angeles took an hour and a half. It was a clear night, with the moon shining brightly, and we could see for miles. About ten minutes before we were due to land, somebody yelled, "Look—look at those cars."

Below us, as far as we could see, were long lines on the freeway, all headed for the airport. As we approached it, we could see more lines coming in the other direction—south from San Francisco. Traffic both ways had stopped completely, and stalled cars jammed up the roads to and from the administration building as well.

Then we heard the pilot's voice. "I'm sorry, boys," he said, "but we can't land until they clear the field. There must be fifty or seventy-five thousand people down there."

We began circling, and pretty soon we heard that the crowds were so close to the runways they didn't dare let any planes take off or land because they were afraid someone might get hurt. We circled for so long we wondered where we would end up. But after an hour and twenty minutes, they finally let us come down at the United Air Lines maintenance runway, about a mile north of the airport. Although there was some confusion picking up luggage and meeting families, we got away without any serious problems. I felt sorry for all those fans milling around, but there was no alternative but to get the boys out of there as quickly and as quietly as possible. With the World Series facing them the next day, they had to go home and get some sleep.

The World Series means a complete personality change for the announcer who broadcasts it. He can be a home team rooter during the regular season, because that's what his listeners are, and they want him to react as they do. But a World Series audience is national. Many listeners don't pay much attention to baseball the rest of the year, and the vast majority don't have strong feelings about either team. All they want is a reporting job, and no one was in a better mood than I to give them one.

I had just seen the Giants pull their second miracle in twelve years, and I was squeezed dry emotionally. While I hoped for the sake of my friends on the team they would collect the winner's share, I didn't really care. They had won the pennant, and that was enough for me.

Of course, I was tempted to yell, "Bye bye baby" when Willie McCovey hit his seventh-inning homer in the second game, and more tempted when Chuck Hiller hit his grand slam in the seventh inning of the fourth. I was delighted to see Jack Sanford win the second game. He had had a sixteen-game streak and piled up a 24-7 winning and losing record during the season. And I was thrilled to see Billy Pierce come back to win the sixth game at Candlestick Park, where he had won twelve in a row during the pennant race.

But, not expecting the Giants to win the Series, I didn't get excited at first. It was only after they tied it up at three games each, with everything riding on the last one at Candlestick, that my nerves started playing tricks on me. I spent a sleepless night before the game, and was all in a sweat the next day.

I was working with my old sidekick, Mel Allen, for the first time since my days with the Yankees. Before the seventh game of the Series, we had a conference with Tom Gallery, the sports director of the National Broadcasting Company, and Perry Smith, the producer of the show. It was decided that I would do the first four and a half innings and Mel the last, but that the announcer whose team was ahead would leave for the clubhouse in the top of the ninth.

Both pitchers were terrific. Ralph Terry of the Yankees had a perfect game until Sanford singled off him with two out in the sixth. McCovey tripled in the seventh and got no further, so Terry had a two-hit shutout by the end of the eighth. In the meantime, the only run the Yankees got off Sanford was on a double play in the fifth. They were leading, 1–0, when it was time to head for the locker room.

Allen left the booth and I took over for him, but with the game that close, we had to provide for the possibility of the Giants' winning. Lon Simmons went to their clubhouse, and was ready to cover it while waiting for me in case the Giants pulled it out.

They nearly did. O'Dell, who had relieved Sanford, held the Yankees hitless in their half of the ninth, so it was still 1–0 when the Giants came to bat. When Matty Alou, batting for O'Dell, beat out a bunt, Candlestick Park started coming alive, and I steeled myself to talk like a reporter instead of a fan. It didn't look as if I'd have to worry about that when Felipe Alou and Hiller both fanned, but then Mays, hitless all day, banged one along the right-field line for a double. Alou stopped at third, because he probably would have been nailed if he had tried to score, and Willie McCovey came up.

He had homered off Terry in the second game, and had tripled in this one. First base was open and McCovey, representing a meaningless run, could have been passed intentionally. Manager Ralph Houk of the Yankees went out to the mound to give Terry his choice of pitching to McCovey or Cepeda, the next batter. Terry decided to take his chances on McCovey.

My heart jumped right into my mouth when McCovey apparently hit the first pitch cleanly, but he pulled it too much and the ball went foul into deep right. Willie took the next pitch, making the count one and one, then got set for the one after. Terry stretched, glanced over at Alou on third, took a quick look at Mays on second, and pitched.

McCovey brought his bat around and there was a roar as the ball shot on a line between first and second base. But before I could open my mouth, Bobby Richardson, the great Yankee second baseman, bent low to his left and grabbed it for the third out.

The Series was over and the Yankees had won. But the Giants forced them right to the last out of the seventh game, and had the tying run on third base and the winning run on second when it ended. If McCovey's shot had gone one more inch to the right, the Giants would have transformed another impossibility into reality. But that shouldn't surprise me, for I ought to know after all these years that the Giants are the miracle-workers of baseball.

And that's not all they are.

They're a San Mateo housewife listening for "Bye bye baby," and an airline ticket agent sticking pins into a Dodger doll. They're Hank Thompson calling Leo Durocher "Lippy," and Harvey Kuenn making a kid run out his hits. They're John McGraw's iron hand and Bill Rigney's felt one and Mel Ott's warmth and Alvin Dark's conscience. They're Eddie Stanky's waving arms and Willie Mays' flying cap. They're Doc Bowman's corn on the cob and Dusty Rhodes' friend Ack-Ack and Sam Jones' toothpicks, and a home run by Bobby Thomson that will live as long as baseball. They're Eddie Brannick's memories and Mrs. McGraw's corsage. They're Felipe Alou and his kid brothers, and Billy Pierce's good left arm. They're Carl Hubbell's screwball and Sal Maglie's control and Orlando Cepeda's power. They're strutting pheasants and fighting cocks and Dalmatian dogs and scared rabbits and ridiculous little gadgets that go "n-n-n-N-N-N-." They're Matty Schwab's hose and Franklin Mieuli's contact lenses. They're Horace Stoneham's hopes and Chub Feeney's fears and San Francisco's heart.

They're Powell Street cable cars and Fifth Avenue buses. They're the Golden Gate and Hell Gate, Market Street and Broadway, Grant Avenue and Mott Street, Russian Hill and Morningside Heights, Candlestick Park and the Polo Grounds, Union Square and Times Square, the Coit Tower and Grant's Tomb, the Embarcadero and West Street, Fisherman's Wharf and Fulton Street. They're the New York that was and the San Francisco that is.

And they're a big Indian and a little fat man in a boar's nest full of maniacs.

They're mine, all mine, and I love them.

My Giants . . .